The Best Places
To Kiss
In Hawaii

"*The Best Places To Kiss* offers more venues from hotels to nightclubs and parks suitably inspiring for good smooching."
New York Daily News

"Our hearts went pit-a-pat when we received our kissing guide."
The New Yorker

"Setting out to find the most romantic places is a humanitarian endeavor you can't afford to ignore."
New York Newsday

"More delightful travel hints abound in *The Best Places To Kiss*. Be sure to include this one in your travel collection."
San Francisco Examiner

"No matter how distant or exotic the destination, you will find it in this beguiling book."
The Toronto Star

"Never has a travel book had so much heart-stirring fun cover-to-cover."
Santa Rosa Press Democrat

"If you need a place for that special occasion, you are sure to find what your hearts need inside."
Oakland Tribune

Other Books in *THE BEST PLACES TO KISS*... Series

The Best Places To Kiss In The Northwest $12.95

The Best Places To Kiss In Southern California........... $10.95

The Best Places To Kiss In Northern California $10.95

The Best Places To Kiss In And Around New York City..... $13.95

The Best Places To Kiss In New England $13.95

Any of these books can be ordered directly from the publisher.

Please send a check or money order for the total amount of the books, plus $1.50 for shipping and handling per book ordered, to:

Beginning Press
5418 South Brandon
Seattle, Washington 98118

Or call (800) 831-4088 for charge card orders.

The Best Places To Kiss In Hawaii

by
Paula Begoun, Stephanie Bell, and Elizabeth Janda

Beginning Press

Art Direction and Production: Lasergraphics
Cover Design: Patrick Howe
Typography: Lasergraphics
Editor: Miriam Bulmer
Printing: Bookcrafters

First Edition: August 1993
1 2 3 4 5 6 7 8 9 10

Best Places To Kiss™ is a registered trademark of Beginning Press
ISBN 1-877988-08-1

This book is distributed to the U.S. book trade by:
Publisher's Group West
4065 Hollis Street
Emeryville, CA 94608
(800) 788-3123

This book is distributed to the Canadian book trade by:
Raincoast Books
112 East Third Avenue
Vancouver, British Columbia V5T 1C8
Canada
(604) 873-6581

Special Acknowledgment

To Avis Begoun, for her extremely creative and romantic original idea for this book, and to all our significant others, who helped us hone our craft.

"In delay there lies no plenty;
Then come kiss me, sweet and twenty,
Youth's a stuff will not endure."

William Shakespeare

Publisher's Note

Travel books have many different formats and criteria for the places they include. We would like the reader to know that this book is not an advertising vehicle. As is true in all the **Best Places To Kiss** books, none of the businesses included here were charged fees, nor did they pay us for their review. This book is a sincere effort to highlight those special parts of the region that are filled with romance and splendor. Sometimes these places were created by people, as in restaurants, inns, lounges, lodges, hotels, and bed and breakfasts. Sometimes these places are untouched by people and simply created by G-d for us to enjoy.

Wherever you go, be gentle with each other and gentle with the earth.

> *"Women still remember the first kiss*
> *after men have forgotten the last."*
> Remy de Gourmont

We Would Love to Hear From You
and Send You a Free Book

The recommendations in this collection were the final decision of the publisher, but we would love to hear what you think of our suggestions. It is our desire to be a reliable source for your amorous outings, and, in this quest for blissful sojourns, your romantic feedback assists greatly in increasing our accuracy and resources for information. Please feel free to write Beginning Press if you have any additional comments, criticisms, or cherished memories of your own from a place we directed you to or of a place you discovered on your own. If we use your information, we will send you a free kissing book of your choice.

Beginning Press
5418 South Brandon
Seattle, WA 98118

*"You are always new.
The last of your kisses was ever the sweetest..."*
John Keats

TABLE OF CONTENTS

"Soul meets soul on lovers' lips."

Percy Bysshe Shelley

The Fine Art of Kissing, Hawaii-Style

Why It's Best To Kiss in Hawaii

Hawaii is not only an exceptionally desirable place to kiss, it is one of *the* premier places to kiss in the world. For those of you who have never been to Hawaii, let me start by telling you it is without question a true tropical paradise. When you first see these jewel-like atolls, it takes very little effort to imagine it as it appeared to the first non-native visitors to these islands over two centuries ago: unspoiled jade green hills and azure blue waves stretching before you in all their majestic remote glory. Today, Western and Eastern cultures have done much to change the flawless appearance of these islands, but the quintessential splendor and legendary scenery are still there in great abundance.

Paradise doesn't often mix well with modernization, and Hawaii has suffered large-scale development by both Japanese and American corporations over the past 20 years, with the greatest influx in just the past five years. Through the 1950s, when the most prized hotel rooms rented for about $10 a night and "The Beach at Waikiki" was a popular song, the islands were still relatively unmarred. Much of that had to do with accessibility. To put it mildly, the Hawaiian Islands are out in the middle of nowhere: 2,400 miles from the nearest coast (equidistant between Japan and the west coast of the United States). Visiting these Polynesian playgrounds meant a long, arduous journey.

Times have changed. Easy access from nearly every corner of the globe makes Hawaii one of the most touristed locales in the world, with the preponderance of visitors coming from the U.S. mainland and Japan. Between 7 million and 8 million vacationers a year come here searching for a taste of tropical heaven. Frequent-flyer award programs and enticing, reasonably priced vacation packages make Hawaii an affordable destination. A week's stay at a hotel or condominium, including car and round-trip airfare from the West Coast to the island of Oahu, can cost as little as $485 per person. With deals like that, the islands' distant, exotic personality at times seems little more than a memory.

It takes some effort to find the truly enchanted, idyllic side of these South Sea islands, but it can be done. In those special places, the kissing will be as amorous as you ever dreamed possible.

The Islands

There are six major islands in the Hawaiian archipelago that you can and should consider visiting for remarkably romantic sojourns. Of these, the big four, from south to north, are the big island of Hawaii, renowned for the volcanic activity of Kilauea; Maui, home to the overdeveloped but exquisite Kaanapali coast and growing tourism; the bustling island of Oahu, boasting the major city of Honolulu and the most well-known beach in the world—Waikiki; and Kauai, a late bloomer as a worthy destination, with additional catching up to do after the disastrous repercussions of Hurricane Iniki. Less known and vastly less developed, the islands of Molokai and Lanai, nestled in a rain shadow between Oahu and Maui, provide the ultimate in authentic tropical seclusion; their gentle spirit is evident from the moment you arrive.

Two other small islands complete the lineup. Nihau, just southwest of Kauai, is privately owned and restricted. Helicopter flights to isolated parts of the island are offered, but interaction with the natives is strictly prohibited, and the lack of amenities, expense of the flight, and minimal local cooperation make it a pricey, joyless getaway. There is little real reason to go apart from fascination with its quarantined status.

The tiny island of Kahoolawe lies slightly southwest of Maui. For decades the army and the navy used it as a target for testing and training their bombers and pilots, which rendered the land desolate and virtually unhabitable. Efforts are now being made to restore and develop the island, but how, when, and by whom is unknown.

How do you choose which island to go to? There are several options for those interested in experiencing everything these islands have to offer. You can settle on just one destination, selecting a particularly romantic place to stay and embrace for your entire visit, or you can just as easily island hop. If you haven't been to Hawaii before, your first inclination may be to start on the island of Oahu. Although we feel that Oahu has the fewest romantic possibilities, you may be tempted to see this well-touristed destination for yourselves. If you do choose to visit Oahu, it is our recommendation to go there first. The most popular of the islands and the most densely populated, it can be a jarring place to end your vacation after spending time on the comparatively more tranquil islands of Kauai, Maui, Lanai, or Molokai. Peace and quiet are not the order of the day for Honolulu or Waikiki. However, if abundant nightlife, the excitement of city streets, and chock-full beaches are part of your idea of romance, whenever you schedule Oahu will be just fine. If a more relaxed, peaceful vacation, away from the bustling masses, is what the two of you are searching for, head for any of the islands *but* Oahu.

Getting Around

There is easy access between the islands via airplane and, for some of the islands located only a few miles apart, via passenger-only ferryboats. Three airlines provide all interisland air service: **Hawaiian Airlines**, (800) 367-5320; **Aloha Airlines**, (800) 367-5250; and **Aloha Island Air**, (800) 323-3345. Passenger ferry service is available from Maui to Lanai via **Expeditions**, (808) 661-3756, and from Maui to Molokai via the **Maui Princess**, (808) 661-8397.

Hawaii's main tourist office, the **Hawaii Visitors Bureau,** is on Oahu. They provide information for all the islands and can be contacted at (808) 923-1811. The phone numbers of the Visitors Bureau on specific islands are as follows: the Big Island of Hawaii, (808) 961-5797; Kauai, (808) 245-3971; and Maui,

(808) 871-8691. The islands of Molokai and Lanai do not have their own Visitors Bureau. For information call the main tourist office on Oahu.

Rental cars are as much a part of the scenery on Hawaii as palm trees, although infinitely less attractive. Without a car, it is all but impossible to experience the shrouded beauty that hides along winding stretches of roads and highways. Once you arrive, you are likely to understand why a rental car is a necessary evil for almost any and all sight-seeing activities that don't involve tours. It is less important to have a car if you plan to stay in Honolulu or near Waikiki, where excellent bus service and taxis are readily available, but even then you may want to consider a day rental here and there to uncover the vistas and scenery of spots less traveled.

There are some great car rental deals to be found, particularly through some of the 100 or so local rental companies, as opposed to the big national chains such as Hertz, Budget, Alamo Rent-A-Car, National-Rent-A-Car, Thrifty and Avis. However, while it is indeed a bargain to book with a local firm, it may not be a great idea to wait until you get here to rent a car, particularly not during high season when there won't be any available. If you want the prices, call a travel agent who can handle it for you or call a few companies on your own, including **Tropical**, (800) 678-6000, and **Payless Car Rental**, (800) 345-5230.

◆   **Romantic Note:** Be sure to check whether the property you are staying at offers a package that includes a car. Many of them do.

The Most Romantic Time To Travel

As impossible as it may seem, Hawaii's beautiful weather doesn't really have an off-season. Although you probably wouldn't want to encourage anyone to visit during the near 90-degree humid heat of July and August, it turns out to be almost as popular a time as the Christmas–New Year holiday season (from December 20 through January 4). Actually, any time school isn't in session is a time when families flock to the islands. In terms of perfection, perhaps the most idyllic weather conditions are to be found during the fall and spring months when the weather is almost always a consistently dry 80 degrees.

Not surprisingly, the most sought after dates in winter are not only the most crowded and most expensive period, they are also dead center of the islands' rainy season. But even during this span you are likely to encounter occasional 68-degree evenings, 75-degree afternoons, and as many sunny days as rainy ones. Conditions on each island can vary. Some sections of the islands are known for their drier conditions and may be preferable during winter. For example, Kapalua and Hana on Maui are the wetter areas of the island in comparison to Wailea, which is more arid; Poipu Beach on Kauai is drier than the Napali Coast; and the east side of Oahu has more rain than the Diamond Head side. Staying in one of those places doesn't mean you won't see rain during the winter months, it just gives you slightly better odds. Schedule your trip with the weather considerations in mind to better create the tropical vacation of your dreams, and not the soaked time off of your nightmares. Or enjoy the rain. Winter may not be sunny but it is usually warm, and the sound of the rain against the palm trees is delightful.

How Important Is Location?

You may be skeptical about the idea that one location is more romantic than another, whether it be Hawaii or your own neighborhood. You may think, "Well, it isn't the setting, it's who you're with that makes a place special." And you'd be right. But aside from the chemistry that exists between the two of you without any help from us, there are some locations that can facilitate and enhance the chemistry, just as there are some that can discourage and frustrate the magic in the moment. More so than any other place we've written about, this can be true for Hawaii. Perhaps it's the romantic expectations of this South Pacific paradise that make it all the more disappointing when a tender embrace is marred by screaming kids, the slamming of car doors, or the noise from an exhaust fan under your private balcony. The very nature of Hawaii's burgeoning high-rise development can become literally *the other side of Eden.* Location isn't everything, but when all the right details are shared by a loving couple, the odds are undeniably better for achieving unhindered and uninterrupted romance.

With that in mind, here is a list of the things that were considered by us to be not even remotely romantic: places with garden or mountain views punctuated by the blare of traffic noise; hotels with impressive lobby and pool areas but mediocre rooms (particularly ones with outrageous price tags); crowded beaches; anything overly plastic or overly veneered; noisy restaurants, even if they were very elegant; most tourist spots (particularly those with facilities for tour buses); discos; the latest to-be-seen-in night spots (romance is looking at each other, not at the people sitting across from you); and row after row of overcrowded condominium developments.

◆ **Romantic Note:** We can't emphasize the following point enough, and you will find it repeated throughout this book. **Many of the brochures and ads for the various hotels, resorts, and restaurants for Hawaii look infinitely better than they are in reality.** We were often shocked (as many unsuspecting tourists have been) at how scintillating the descriptions of a place sounded and how enticing the pictures looked, and then, when we arrived, none of it was evident in even the tiniest corner of the grounds or building. Striving to give candid, genuine reviews is the hallmark of the *Best Places To Kiss* series. We understand how disappointment can affect your ability to pucker up.

Romance Ratings

The three major factors that determined whether a place would be included were:

1. Surrounding splendor
2. Privacy
3. Tug-at-your-heartstrings ambience

Of the three determining factors, "surrounding splendor" and "privacy" are fairly self-explanatory. "Tug-at-your-heartstrings ambience" can probably use some clarification. Ambience, by our definition, is not limited to clean hotel rooms or tables decorated with white tablecloths and nicely folded linen napkins. Added to all that there must be a certain plushness and spaciousness plus other engaging features that encourage intimacy and allow for affectionate discussions. For the most part, ambience was rated according to degree of comfort and number of gracious appointments, as opposed to image and frills.

If a place had all three of the qualities listed above, its inclusion was automatic. If one or two of the criteria were weak or nonexistent, the other feature(s) had to be really incredible before the place could be recommended. For example, if a breathtakingly beautiful viewpoint was situated in an area inundated with tourists and families on vacation, the place would not normally be included. However, if a fabulous hotel was beset with scores of other guests, it was included if, and only if, its interior was so wonderfully inviting and regal that the other guests no longer seemed to matter.

◆ **Romantic Note:** Hawaii is inherently romantic, but it is also a unique tourist destination. Often we found majestic scenery and sensual beaches surrounded by condominium developments and overrun by substantial crowds, or stayed at stupendous resort hotels with 500 rooms—not exactly intimate or private by anyone's standards. Our basic guideline for selecting a specific place for its kissing potential has always been to search out smaller, more intimate, and out-of-the-mainstream spots, particularly when it comes to accommodations. Hawaii caused a distinct departure from our usual modus operandi. We were in a predicament: should we ignore a magnificent setting because of its current popularity or a luxurious hotel because of its size, or should we adapt our standards to the unique attributes of the Hawaiian Islands? Good question. We decided on the latter, and consequently you will read many entries that sound something like "There are too many people for this to be truly romantic but ..." or "This is too large to be genuinely intimate but ..."

Kiss Ratings

If you've flipped through this book and noticed the miniature lips that accompany each entry, you're probably curious about what they represent. Most other travel guides use a star system, among other symbols, to rank the places they write about; for obvious reasons, we have chosen lips. The rating system notwithstanding, all the places listed in this book are considered special places to be; all of them have heart-pleasing considerations and are worthwhile places to visit. The tiny lips indicate only our personal preferences and the grandness of a spot. They are a way of indicating just how delightfully romantic we found a place to be and how pleased we were with the service and environment during our stay. The number of lips awarded each location indicated the following:

Romantic	💋
Magical	💋💋
Almost Irresistible	💋💋💋
Sublime	💋💋💋💋

Cost Ratings

We have also included ratings to help you determine whether your lips can afford to kiss in a particular restaurant, hotel, or bed and breakfast (many of the outdoor places are free or there is a minimal fee for parking and entrance). The price for overnight accommodations is always based on double occupancy; otherwise there wouldn't be anyone to kiss. Eating establishment prices are based on a full dinner for two (appetizer, entrée, and dessert), excluding liquor, unless otherwise indicated. Because prices and business hours change, it is always advisable to call ahead so that your hearts and lips will not end up disappointed.

Most of the accommodations listed in this book have an extensive and diverse price list for their rooms based mostly on the view and the time of year. Our cost rating includes both the lowest and the highest prices available regardless of the season, and is based on a property's published rate. It does not take into account special promotion packages or available upgrades. If you are traveling any time other than high season, you may want to consider booking the least expensive room and asking for an upgrade when you arrive. Most hotels and some condominium rental properties are pleased to do that for you. (It never hurts to ask, but do not even think of upgrading between December 20 and January 15.)

Restaurant Rating

Inexpensive	Under $25
Moderate	$25 to $50
Expensive	$50 to $80
Very Expensive	$80 to $110
Unbelievably Expensive	$110 and up

Lodging Rating

Very Inexpensive	Under $75
Inexpensive	$75 to $90
Moderate	$90 to $125
Expensive	$130 to $175
Very Expensive	$185 to $240
Unbelievably Expensive	$250 and up

◆ **Romantic Note:** There are almost always specials and packages or upgrades to be had. It may take an assertive tourist to locate them, but it definitely beats paying the overpriced published (or "rack") rate.

Romance in a Condominium

Unlike any other vacation spot you will ever visit, the number of condominiums available for rent in Hawaii is nothing less than staggering. Reviewing these properties was literally a frightening, albeit necessary, task. There are great advantages to staying in a condominium complex: they are generally much less expensive than the larger resort hotels; there are no extra costs such as service people to tip, phone surcharges, or pricey mini-bar treats; and they often have hotel-style front desk check-in and service. Condominiums also offer more space, fully equipped kitchens where meals can be cooked (saving the cost of repeatedly eating out), and separate dining and living room areas.

What are the negatives? Other than the lack of porters and concierges, truly none. Of course, not all condominium complexes are created equal. Some pile people on top of each other like sardines, while others have no air-conditioning—a definite draw-back on hot, breezeless nights. They tell you that the trade winds cool things off, but I assure you it isn't always so. Also, because the condominiums in rental pools are privately owned, the furnishings can vary from luxurious to tacky.

The best prices for a condominium stay are to be found on Oahu ($80 to $100 and up a night), while Maui condo rentals can start at $120 for just average properties. We've done most of the searching for you, but if you are traveling on a package and do not find the property you have been given listed in this book, be sure to stipulate categorically the type of unit you want or don't want (phone, air-conditioning, view, exact distance to a sandy beach, accessible jogging path, available maid service, near a main road, no traffic noise, or anything else that might be important to your stay) and *get it in writing*. Do not risk a spoiled vacation by finding yourselves with disappointing accommodations.

Consider the following as potential questions to ask when attempting to rent a condominium:

- How far are you from the airport?
- How far *exactly* is the nearest beach and is it safe for swimming and snorkeling?
- If there's a view from the unit, how much view is there?
- Is there anything obstructing the view and if so, what?
- What size beds are provided?
- How far is the property from any other activity you are personally interested in, like golf, nightlife, restaurants, or grocery stores?
- Is maid service provided?
- Is air conditioning and/or a phone provided?
- Is a car rental part of the package?

◆ **Romantic Note:** Speaking of condominiums, at some point during your visit in Hawaii you are very likely to receive a sales pitch from a time-share salesperson. In exchange for sitting through one of their presentations you will be offered a one-day free rental car, a dinner sail, a visit to a wax museum, or some other attraction (many of which are not very romantic or even very interesting). There is a great deal of consumer information about time-shares you should know before you deal with a provocative sales performance (and I mean provocative). Do your homework before you inadvertently get involved with something you may be better off resisting.

Romance in a Bed and Breakfast, Hawaii-Style

Unlike areas on the mainland, professionally run bed and breakfasts are hard to find in Hawaii. It's not that they don't exist, it's just that the vast majority of them are represented exclusively by bed-and-breakfast agencies and these companies don't make it easy for travel writers (they are very protective of giving out names and numbers without a booking). Also, licensing is very complicated and political, so a vast number of bed and breakfasts are run illegally. Additionally, most bed and breakfasts don't advertise, and only a handful are listed in the phone book. That means we often couldn't scope out a property before booking. Booking and then assessing is a highly inefficient way to weed through literally hundreds of bed and breakfasts. Usually we seek out only the best and then book before we do a final review for inclusion. Given the number of listings, with descriptions that often sounded infinitely better than they actually were, it would take an amazing amount of time to distinguish between the merely funky and the luxurious if staying were the only way to discover that.

Bed and breakfast Hawaii-style is more informal (and vastly less expensive) than what you may be used to in, say, New England or northern California. Many of the hosts work at other jobs, have families, or are retired, and it can feel more like a home stay with a relative than anything else. But a wide variety of accommoda-

tions are available—everything from separate cottages to apartments located on your own floor of an oceanfront home. We did
our best to uncover as many of the more professionally run,
comfortable, and plush places as we could. Given the limited
number we've included, for those who prefer bed-and-breakfast
accommodations (something we wholeheartedly endorse) using a
local agency is the primary way to go. Be specific about your
requirements, expectations, and needs, and get it in writing. Your
lips will be eternally thankful if you do.

◆   **Romantic Note:** The only bed-and-breakfast agency we
found that had consistently high standards for the properties it
chose to represent on all the islands was **HAWAII'S BEST BED
AND BREAKFAST,** (808) 885-0550.

A Room with a View

Incredibly sensual views abound in Hawaii, and the vision of
sun-drenched, opalescent blue beaches can be enough to fill your
heads and hearts with anticipation even before you start packing.
Most people go to Hawaii with the expectation of partaking in as
much of the aforementioned spectacles as possible. It isn't surpris-
ing to discover that the better the view and the proximity to the
water, the steeper the increase in the rate of your room. Most hotels
add sizable increments for every floor and corner as the view im-
proves from a peekaboo glimpse of the Pacific to the most coveted
possession, a full frontal, unobstructed vista of the rolling surf. Be
aware that sometimes an expensive ocean view is above a noisy
pool, between thick foliage, way off in the distance, or over a massive rooftop. When you ask for a specific room, make your request
and get an answer in writing. Do not settle for the words "ocean
view" on your confirmation. There is a lot of leeway in that descrip-
tion, and that could set you up for a burn that isn't from the sun.

Is a room with a view necessary? That depends on your budget
and preferences. Many lovely properties that have minimal water
views or a magnificent mountain view (sans cars) with a beach
nearby are wonderful places to stay. But it would be misleading to
say that waking to the sound of the waves surging against the shore
and a view of the endless oceans isn't more romantic and breath-

taking, because it is. Balancing quality of accommodations against view and beach accessibility was one of the major objectives in all our reviews concerning accommodations.

◆ **Romantic Warning:** Expensive doesn't always mean most desirable, and well-known hotel properties can have their drawbacks, such as a mountain or garden view highlighted by a well-trafficked street or parking lot, or rooms in need of renovation. Read our recommendations carefully; sometimes reputations die hard, which can make for some lackluster kissing places.

Love Among the Golf Courses

Almost as big a draw as the beaches and exquisite scenery are the assortment of world-class golf courses in Hawaii. Set on hillsides, bordering the ocean, wrapped around premier resort properties, these links make the islands a golfer's utopia. Golf tournaments abound, golf carts circle about in the distance, and you are as likely to overhear conversations discussing the layout of a course and the great shots of the day as praise for the beautiful beaches. This book is not about golfing, but we would be remiss not to mention this attraction for affectionate couples who together or separately may want to go for one or more under par. All of the islands have several excellent courses to choose from. To get more information about golf courses in Hawaii, call the **Hawaii Visitors Bureau** at (808) 923-1811. Even if you are not fond of golf, these courses are so magnificent that you may find yourself drawn to this sport that has so many island visitors firmly under its spell.

Getting Married in Hawaii

Many of the more notable island hotels increasingly specialize in weddings and renewals of vows. It would be fairly typical for you to encounter brides and grooms in full regalia at many of the major resorts; some of them handle more than 60 weddings a month. These noteworthy vacation packages are gaining popularity because the hotels make it so easy for you and they can be surprisingly affordable. Some resorts have romance directors or wedding organizers whose sole job is attending to the details of your nuptials, no matter how simple or complex the event. If you do decide to utilize the exotic surroundings of Hawaii for the most romantic interlude of your life, there are plenty of options available. Simply find the hotel of your choice in the listings that follow and ask for their wedding or romance planner, tell them your budget, and they'll take it from there. It is really that simple.

To Luau or Not To Luau?

More luaus take place on the Hawaiian Islands today than ever took place in all of the islands' combined pre-statehood history. Every major hotel and even some minor ones as well as large and small restaurants host luaus on a nightly basis. There are even special restaurants with incredible outside settings dedicated only to luaus. No matter which one(s) you choose to attend, you will behold a totally contrived, artificial reenactment of a once time-honored Hawaiian ritual. The rampant commercialism of this tradition has destroyed whatever authenticity might have existed. In spite of our recommendation to avoid a luau, the lure to attend at least one will be hard to resist. Go for it. Although one should be enough. You will find the dancing colorful enough, the music quite entertaining (although performance quality varies greatly), and the traditional *imu* (a whole pig cooked in an underground pit) very good, but those are the high points. The dinner is served buffet-style, which means a large crowd lining up at the same time for usually mediocre food (including coleslaw, potato salad, overly sweet punch, and standard white cake with frosting). It isn't very Hawaiian, but it's not all that easy to find the *real* Hawaii anymore. We do recommend a few luaus, but these are only halfhearted recommendations. The wholehearted recommendations are for only the most truly romantic Hawaiian experiences.

◆　**Romantic Note:** The only thing more abundant in Hawaii than condos and luaus are sight-seeing activities. The possibilities are almost overwhelming. We have highlighted the best (and worst) excursions to consider for each individual island. When it comes to outdoor tours, it is difficult to make a mistake. As long as it involves the water or gloriously scenic sights, the only negative may be the crowds; the water and vistas will be just as you hoped—ecstatically awesome. Cultural centers and museums also offer a colorful, insightful perspective of life in Hawaii throughout the generations. Take advantage of these whenever you can. Although they can often feel like tourist traps, the information is intriguing and thought provoking.

Surf's Up

Please read this section carefully together. Water safety can never be emphasized too much. Just ask any hospital emergency room staffer in Hawaii about respect for the powers of the ocean. The water beckons with a siren's call that cannot be ignored, and the desire to rush hand-in-hand out into the surf will be intense, absolute, and easy to do with nary a wince or shrug: after all, the water temperature is an optimal 75 to 80 degrees year-round. The brilliant blues of the water can mask the turbulence and force of the surf and tides. Although the ocean may appear calm or flat when you enter, moments later you are likely to confront a crashing set of waves that can tumble you out of control back onto the beach. The following are specific guidelines to consider whenever you want to act out your own *From Here To Eternity* beach scene:

- ◆ Waves come in sets, and even though all you presently see are small waves, bigger ones may be on the way.
- ◆ Never turn your back on the ocean. Watch for what is coming your way.
- ◆ If you do encounter a breaking wave, do not try to outswim it or ride it ashore. Your best option is to duck or dive under it. The waves pass over you rather quickly, but be ready, the next one is on its way.
- ◆ Remember that tidal undertow can pull you farther out than you want to go.
- ◆ Never swim alone (besides, alone isn't romantic).
- ◆ If you can't swim, do not play in high, rolling waves. At first the water may seem only knee-deep but it can become 15 feet deep in the blink of an eye.

◆ Distances in the water can be deceiving. Judge your endurance conservatively.

◆ Do not step on coral reefs (coral cuts are painful and can become infected) or on rocky ground where sea urchins and eel bites are prevalent.

◆ It is best to watch surfers from high ground. Avoid being in the water at the same time with a group of surfers if you are not savvy to surfer etiquette. You can easily get hit by a surfer or a runaway surfboard.

◆ There are sharks in these waters, but they prefer fish to humans. Shark attacks are infrequent and rarely result in a fatality. If you do see a shark, do not panic; swim quietly away, get out of the water, and tell a lifeguard of your sighting.

◆ **Romantic Note:** When you are snorkeling, the temptation to remove some of the sea's alluring natural gifts can be hard to resist, but be strong. The ocean is not a gift shop, and what you remove is not easily replaced. Be respectful of nature's wonders and leave them there for the next couple to enjoy.

◆ **Second Romantic Note: Remember, all beaches in Hawaii are public** and are some of the most spectacular in the world. They are often somewhat difficult to access around the massive hotel properties and private homes here, but they are accessible. No beach can be privately owned; they are all available for use by everyone. Signage may not be visible or exist at all, but that doesn't mean you can't use the beach.

Sunscreen: Don't Leave Home Without It

Nothing can destroy a romantic holiday or your ability to kiss faster than a sunburn, and the Hawaiian sun can burn fast and furiously. If you pack nothing else you need to pack a sunscreen with an SPF (sun protection factor) of at least 12 to 15. It doesn't have to be expensive as long as it has a high SPF rating. (Because of FDA regulations, all sunscreens protect from the sun equally based on the SPF number.) For total protection from both UVA and UVB rays (broad spectrum protection), you may want to consider a nonchemical sunscreen. Not only do these new sunscreens provide more protection, they are also virtually irritant-free. No more burning eyes. Look for the words "chemical free" or "nonchemical" on the label if you are interested in this type of protection.

Be sure to apply sunscreen at least 20 minutes before you go out in the sun. You can get burned just in the time it takes to walk from your car to the beach and spread out your blanket. Apply sunscreen evenly and generously, covering every inch of exposed skin. Don't forget the tops of your feet, thin hair spots, the hairline, parts, ears, and eyelids. It is also essential to reapply sunscreen after you swim or exercise. Try to purchase a sunscreen before your departure: the hotels and stores in Hawaii charge a hefty fee in comparison to what you would pay in a drugstore on the mainland.

What To Pack

As many times as we've been to Hawaii, we still engage in a never-ending discussion about what we should and shouldn't pack. It seems self-evident, yet it is of great concern given the variety of experiences and attractions available and the inevitable heat. Obviously a lot depends on your itinerary, but there are some basics to help lighten your luggage.

Be assured that shorts and a short-sleeved shirt of any kind are acceptable at 99 percent of the places you will visit. Even tank tops for both women and men are fine in most casual restaurants and shops. We were often surprised at what is considered acceptable. These islands have an amazingly nonchalant, laid-back temperament. However, the dress code does change when you are off for a more posh evening of dining and dancing. Many of the finer restaurants require women to wear nice resort wear and men to wear long sleeves and jackets. But don't worry about bringing a jacket along—almost all of the fancier restaurants have jackets you can borrow while you dine and some are much less strict than their policy implies. If you choose to attend a luau or other evening entertainment, the dress depends on the type of place. The fancier the venue, the more clothes you have to wear.

During the winter months the nights can get a bit on the cool side. For Hawaii that means in the low 70s or high 60s. A lightweight cotton sweater or jacket is all you should need to ward off the slight evening chill. Cotton slacks are also a good idea on those occasions.

In terms of what to wear for bedtime, it just depends on what he buys you and what you buy him.

◆ **Romantic Note:** We always pack our own snorkels, fins, and beach towels so we can indulge our urge for the surf at a moment's notice without worrying about rentals. But don't be concerned if you don't have your own; there are plenty of rental places all over the islands.

Whale Watching

If you have always secretly longed to witness firsthand the passage of whales on their yearly migration to warmer waters (when the hump-back whales give birth to their young), then the Hawaiian Islands are a great place to live out your underwater fantasy. December to April is the best time to witness this odyssey, particularly when the weather conditions are clear and sunny. Be sure to start your search early, about the time when the sun is radiantly warming the cooler morning air. As you stand at the edge of the shore scanning the Pacific realm, you will have a tremendous view of the open waters. Find a comfortable sandy spot or grassy knoll, snuggle close together, and be patient. This performance is intermittent at best and requires careful inspection and diligence. But be prepared for an amazing encounter.

Imagine: You are slowly studying the calm, azure waters. Then suddenly, in the distance, breaking the still of a silent, sun-drenched Hawaiian winter morning, a spout of bursting water explodes from the surface. A giant, arched black profile appears boldly against the blue sea, followed by an abrupt tail slap and then stillness once more. It's hard to explain the romance of that moment, but romantic it is. Perhaps it's the excitement of observing such an immense creature gliding effortlessly through the water with playful agility and ease. Or perhaps it's the chance to celebrate a part of nature's mysterious aquatic underworld together. Whatever it is, discover it for yourselves if you have the chance.

◆ **Romantic Note:** There are good viewpoints for whale watching from numerous spots on many of the islands, but it is particularly prime off the southern shores of Maui. There are also boat excursions that can take you out for more intimate viewing from all the islands. On Maui the most enlightening whale watching cruises are sponsored by the **PACIFIC WHALE WATCHING FOUNDATION**, (808) 879-8811 or (800) WHALE-11. Daily departures are from Maalaea Harbor and Lahaina Harbor. Your guides are authorities from the foundation and fill the two-and-a-half-hour expedition with everything you ever wanted to know about whales and more.

A Brief History

Hawaii's distinctly separate identity and distance from the mainland gives it the feeling of being part of a culture other than the United States, but it was associated with the U.S. even before it became the 50th state in 1959. Beginning about A.D. 1200, when the first Polynesian (believed to be Tahitian) settlers first arrived on these islands, and culminating in the multibillion-dollar tourist industry of today, Hawaii's history is a fascinating and spellbinding saga. Although often characterized as a peaceful, untroubled corner of the world before missionaries and colonists came bringing sickness, Western religion, and capitalism, that is not a totally accurate or complete depiction. Before the European discovery of these islands by Captain Cook in 1788, the tribes on the islands were continually at war, vying for position and dominance; human sacrifice was a customary religious practice; and there was a caste system (*kapu*) in place that made life miserable for some and luxurious for others.

It wasn't until the arrival of Western civilization that human sacrifice was stopped, the *kapu* system was eliminated, and the population was educated. Western civilization also changed the unspoiled glory of the land forever, creating intense foreign commerce with whaling in the 1840s, agriculture in the form of sugar and pineapple plantations in the 1850s and 1860s, and the elaborate and virtually overflowing tourist industry of the present.

Perhaps the most notorious and controversial interaction between the United States and Hawaii occurred in 1893, when Queen Liliuokalani, after trying to reinstate her rightful control over the islands, was overthrown by American Republican forces in Honolulu. Seven years later Hawaii became a territory of the United States, and the monarchy was officially defunct.

Over the past 20 years the plantation fields of pineapple and sugar cane have slowly lost their financial productivity and been superseded by high-rise hotels and condominiums. Almost all of the local population to one degree or another, directly or indirectly, works for the massive tourist industry.

From ancient Polynesians crossing the oceans more than 800 years ago to the jam-packed streets of Waikiki today, there is much to discover regarding the history of Hawaii. We encourage you to take the time to delve more into this remarkable chronicle. It would be a shame to come all this way and not find the real Hawaii, because it does exist, not on the beaches or at tourist attractions, but in the history books.

Oahu

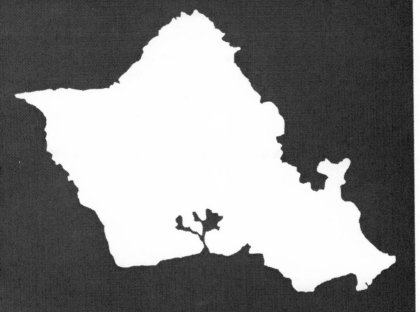

> *"Oh, they loved dearly; their souls kissed,*
> *they kissed with their eyes,*
> *they were both but one single kiss!"*
>
> Heinrich Heine

OAHU

No two better words describe the second-largest of the Hawaiian Islands than agony and ecstasy. It is clearly an island of contrasts; in the south-shore area of Waikiki they really did "pave paradise and put up a parking lot," not to mention busy streets, enormous high-rise hotels, shopping centers, jewelry stores, and more jewelry stores. All of this development services millions of tourists a year who want their own taste of tropical bliss and utopian paradise eclipsed by steel-girded urban sprawl. Sigh. On the other side of this concrete jungle is the famous beach at Waikiki, with its vast aqua blue shallow waters and white sand, not to mention nearly perfect year-round temperatures. Yes, the beach and weather are gorgeous, but Oahu is so densely covered with tourists (about 80,000 daily on average) that it isn't anyone's idea of paradise anymore.

You can escape the crowds to some degree by heading east to **DIAMOND HEAD**, where the hotels thin out and turn into elite residential areas. The sandy beaches here are gorgeous (one is even called **SANDY BEACH**) but popular with local surfers, which doesn't leave you much privacy. Still, crowds are definitely less dense than at Waikiki, which can be a considerable kissing advantage. There isn't much else on the island with an atmosphere resembling paradise, at least nothing where there are also accommodations readily available. Prime snorkeling can be found at **HANAUMA BAY**, but it isn't a secret, and the area can spill over with sea-life enthusiasts.

Sunsets on the northwest shore are extraordinary, and you can park your car and walk along any number of sandy beaches, **SUNSET BEACH** and **WAIMEA BEACH** in particular, to enjoy the tropical scenery. These areas are also celebrated surfing spots with awesome, crashing waves. Farther south, near **KAENA POINT STATE PARK,** majestic scenery abounds and a formidable surf crashes against rocks interspersed with patches of sand. Be forewarned that although these areas are primarily residential and undeveloped (sans hotels and condominiums), much of it is run-down and you're likely to run across communes of makeshift houses scattered along the coast.

Head north for a beautiful drive between the **WAINAE AND KOOLAU MOUNTAIN RANGES** that rise majestically on either side of you. The north shore itself is again primarily residential, but remember that *all* of the beaches on the island are public (even if they look private), so keep your eyes open for access paths. The coast is heavily dotted with houses, but you might get lucky and find a beach all to yourselves. Even if you don't, you're sure to find fewer crowds than you would in Waikiki.

Popular locations such as the 1,800-acre **WAIMEA FALLS PARK,** (808) 923-8448, and the **POLYNESIAN CULTURAL CENTER,** (808) 293-3333, provide interesting day trips, but the crowds and theme park atmosphere leave romantic urges cold.

◆   **Romantic Note:** Although we don't often recommend tourist attractions, we urge you to take the time to see the **ARIZONA MEMORIAL**. Poignant and affecting, it is dedicated to the U.S. military lives lost during World War II's Pearl Harbor attack.

Waikiki

It probably isn't best to kiss on the beach at Waikiki, because if you close your eyes for a moment and move ever so slightly, you may end up kissing someone you don't know. The shoulder-to-shoulder lineup of bodies on a warm day is staggering. However, at night, when the crowds are across the street shopping at the endless promenade of stores and markets, this warm and exquisite beach is practically private.

Hotel/Bed and Breakfast Kissing

ASTON WAIKIKI BEACH TOWER, Waikiki
2470 Kalakaua Avenue
(808) 926-6400
Expensive

On Kalakaua Avenue on the west end of Waikiki.

Exotic white flowers cover an enclosed, trellised walkway, drawing you into this small but exquisite hotel. It's easy to bypass this small diamond in the rough, hiding in the midst of several sky-rise hotels. Although the beach is just across the street, Kalakaua Avenue is heavily trafficked and detracts from its allure. Nevertheless, koa wood, hand-painted Asian antiques, a beautifully detailed wall mural, and bouquets of exotic flowers found in the handsome lobby are telltale clues to the luxury that awaits you in the upstairs suites. Although the hallways are dim and drab, the guest suites are spacious and elegant, appointed with modern furnishings and attractive color schemes. Sizable lanais open to views of the ocean, and an ample gourmet kitchen and fully stocked wet bar add to your comfort. The bedrooms are simple yet attractive and also enjoy ocean views (which are better the higher you go, as is the lack of street noise). If you can tear yourselves away from the view, sneak downstairs to splash each other in the outdoor heated pool or whirlpool tub. And don't worry about crowds: this is one of the best kept secrets in this part of town.

ASTON WAIKIKI BEACHSIDE HOTEL, Waikiki
2452 Kalakaua Avenue
(808) 931-2100
Expensive to Very Expensive

On Kalakaua Avenue between Uluniu and Liliuokalani avenues.

In many ways this is one of the most unusual hotel properties you will find on Oahu or on any of the Hawaiian Islands for that matter. Only 77 rooms fill this boutique hotel set directly across the street from the beach. Intimate and cozy, each room features European detailing in pastel peach fabrics and walls, hand-painted Oriental screens, plush furnishings, attractive marble baths, and twice-daily maid service. All in all, the atmosphere is elegant and refined, and you won't find any of the overbearing, impersonal large proportions offered by the countless other hotels lining Waikiki.

◆ **Romantic Warning:** The rooms here, while tasteful, are on the small side, and rooms with numbers ending in 04 and 05 have no windows. Even if those rooms were free you couldn't tolerate it for more than a minute or two.

HAWAIIAN REGENT, Waikiki
2552 Kalakaua Avenue
(808) 922-6611
Moderate to Expensive

From the Honolulu Airport take Highway 1 east to the King Street cutoff to Kapahulu Avenue. After you pass a zoo on the left, turn right onto Kuhio Avenue. Turn left onto Ohua Avenue; the hotel is on the immediate left.

One hundred years ago, Queen Liliuokalani, Hawaii's last reigning monarch, luxuriated and entertained in her summer home, encompassed by the beauty and fragrances of surrounding flower gardens. That site is now the location of the Hawaiian Regent, and you can experience a different kind of sanctuary in this quieter segment of Kalakaua Avenue. Although quiet is relative in Waikiki, the crowds relent somewhat here, even at the beach across the street. The Hawaiian Regent is just a five-minute walk from Waikiki's shopping district and offers ocean views for moderate prices, a welcome alternative to the nearby extravagantly expensive luxury hotels.

Built in 1971, the Regent is sorely overdue for renovations, and fortunately these are in store for 1993. Until then, be aware that the 1,346 (yes, it's huge) guest rooms in both sky-rise towers are dated and sometimes even downright tacky. Even so, unhindered ocean views (especially in the corner rooms), in-room refrigerators, first-class service and amenities, and the Regent's convenient location continue to attract tourists with romantic agendas.

Whatever is lacking in decor is more than compensated for in other areas. Stroll at nightfall through open-air corridors that enclose nicely landscaped courtyards filled with tropical flowers and foliage. Or swim under the stars in either of two swimming pools, one of which has a gorgeous view of the ocean. Championship tennis courts, shopping arcades, and excellent restaurants, not to mention the nearby zoo, aquarium, and sandy beach across the street, ensure that you'll never want for things to do. When the sun has set and you've seen it all, retire to your room to drink in views of the twinkling city lights on the horizon. Fresh orchids left on your pillows by the turndown service are a nice extra touch. Ah, it's the small things in life.

HALEKULANI, Waikiki
2199 Kalia Road
(808) 923-2311
Expensive to Very Expensive

From Kalakaua Avenue, turn toward the water onto Lewers Street. The hotel will be directly in front of you.

Whatever misgivings you have about Waikiki (and there are potentially many) are soon forgotten at the Halekulani. It's really that nice. Halekulani means "house befitting heaven," and in spite of the fact that this luxury hotel is set in the midst of a cluttered beachfront, the name aptly describes what you'll find here. Quiet splendor enfolds you as you step from the nearby busy street into an open-air lobby, replete with ocean views, small waterfall pools, imported marble pillars framing gracious corridors, and conservative but lovely garden landscaping. A beautifully tiled oceanside swimming pool beckons to you, flaunting a brilliant white painted orchid under the shimmering surface of the blue water. The only drawback to this otherwise faultless property is the boardwalk that separates the hotel from the public beach. It serves to keep the wandering locals and tourists out, but interrupts the natural ocean scenery. You can only people watch for so long before you long for an unobstructed view.

All of the 456 guest rooms in the hotel's three looming towers have ocean views from private lanais and are quite possibly the nicest guest rooms to be found in all of Waikiki. Surprisingly, prices here are no more outlandish (although I certainly wouldn't call them reasonable) than most of the other luxury resorts in the area. You are immersed in white the moment you enter your suite, from the plush carpet and crisp bed linens to the sparkling bathroom tiles. Discerning attention to detail adds romantic flair to the mood. Seashells left on your bed and fresh bouquets of exotic flowers embellish the white-on-white decor with streaks of color. In the spacious bathroom, slide open the shutters surrounding the sunken soaking tub to reveal ocean views from the windows of your bedroom. Even by our standards (and admittedly we're skeptics when it comes to Waikiki) this is utter bliss.

Halekulani's two restaurants—the exorbitant, extremely polished and sophisticated **LA MER** and the more casual **ORCHIDS** (both are reviewed elsewhere in this section)—offer efficient, attentive service, unpretentious settings, and a refreshing amount of open-air drama.

HAWAII PRINCE HOTEL, Waikiki
100 Holomoana Street
(808) 956-1111, (800) 321-OAHU
Expensive to Unbelievably Expensive

Call for directions.

Opened with great hoopla and fanfare, the Hawaii Prince Hotel turns out to be not much of a prince. I'm not even sure you could designate it anything more than a mere commoner. Located a fair distance from the hustle of the beach at Waikiki, this newly built high-rise is a strange addition to the multifarious places to stay on Oahu. Facing a quiet marina, it has no nearby beach access and virtually no open-air space to speak of anywhere in the massive complex. The lobby design is quite cold and stark, and throughout the hotel many of the finishing touches seem thrown together. Although new, the paint is already peeling and there are torn moldings in the corners.

The rooms are nicely furnished, but they are also small and confining, and the absence of balconies makes them seem even smaller, bordering on claustrophobic. All in all, the architectural design seems more suitable to New York City than the tropics of Hawaii.

Having suggested quite plainly that the Hawaii Prince may be the last place you want to stay in Hawaii, we must add that it is the premier place to dine. The **PRINCE COURT** restaurant (reviewed elsewhere in this section) serves some of the most remarkable cuisine we tasted on any of the islands.

HILTON HAWAIIAN VILLAGE, Waikiki
2005 Kalia Road
(808) 949-4321, (800) HILTONS
Moderate to Unbelievably Expensive

On the corner of Ala Moana Boulevard and Kalia Road.

You could live here for a month and never have to leave the property. The Hilton is more than a village, it's almost a small city, providing guests with everything from a post office to a beauty salon. (The President and his entourage have even been known to take asylum here.) Situated on 20 acres of prime, but crowded, beachfront property, the Hilton boasts fantastic ocean views from its unbelievable 2,542 guest rooms in four sky-rise towers. In addition to multitudes of shopping boutiques and cafés, the village provides three outdoor swimming pools, seven restaurants, five lounges, and live entertainment such as Charo and the *Magic of Polynesia* show. The "super pool," a 10,000-square-foot pool surrounded by thundering lava rock waterfalls and tropical landscaping, is only an example of the extravagance found throughout the property. The Hilton is the largest resort on all of the Hawaiian Islands, and its vast size can be, to say the least, overwhelming. Intimacy is clearly not the focus.

Of the four towers, the Ali'i Tower is the exclusive concierge tower, offering 348 deluxe guest suites appointed with colonial antiques and Oriental themes. This tower provides guest services ranging from car rental to babysitting and an additional plus: a private health and fitness spa with pool, sauna, whirlpool, and massage rooms. The remaining three towers are less luxurious and provide fewer amenities, but maintain the stately and attractive modern decor.

The sky is the limit at the Hilton. You can relish the tropics in the convenience of a city within a city. But remember, if you're looking to leave city life and crowds behind you, you're in the wrong place.

HYATT REGENCY, Waikiki
2424 Kalakaua Avenue
(808) 923-1234, (800) 233-1234
Expensive to Unbelievably Expensive

From Kalakaua Avenue, turn onto Kaiulani Avenue, turn right on Koa Street, then turn right again on Uluniu Street. The 40-story hotel is on the right. (It's hard to miss.)

Directly across the street from the beach at Waikiki stands this massive twin-towered hotel complex rising 40 stories above the water. Centered around a large atrium lobby with a cascading waterfall, the ground floor is like a shopping mall complex, complete with more jewelry stores than you would even want to count. Despite the gigantic size there are truly some wonderful, spacious rooms here with attractive, comfortable furnishings, and the higher up you go, the closer you are to a bird's-eye view of the scintillating tropical and city scenery. Much below the 20th floor and the noise from astoundingly busy Kalakaua Avenue will not be music to your ears. The higher up you go the better, but even on the 40th floor traffic noise can drift up and invade your privacy.

Of the six restaurants here the only one we would wholeheartedly recommend for affectionate dining is **CIAO MEIN**, set next to the outdoor pool. Fresh air breezes through the casual setting filled with plants and well-spaced tables; the black and white motif is softened with wicker chairs and subtle lighting. The blend of Oriental and Italian cuisine is not always successful, but the classic dishes are all quite good.

MANOA VALLEY INN, Waikiki
2001 Vancouver Drive
(808) 947-6019, (800) 634-5115
Inexpensive

Call for directions.

Bed and breakfasts are rare commodities in Hawaii, and the Manoa Valley Inn is the only historical inn of its kind on Oahu. The three-story gabled country inn set back in a residential neighborhood once reveled in ocean views. Today, Waikiki's high-rise skyline looms instead in the distance, unalluring in the daytime but lovely at night when the city lights emerge in the darkness. Although this view is hardly what you would call paradise, you can enjoy the urban scenery over continental breakfast on the backyard covered lanai and imagine the splendor of the days before the developers moved in.

You'll find this lanai to be the coziest spot for two. The other common rooms are timeworn and almost dreary. You can, however, examine the interesting antiques, including a nickelodeon and antique victrola. The upstairs guest rooms feature more remnants of the past, including weathered black-and-white framed photographs, iron and four-poster beds, patterned wallpaper, and marble-topped dressers, all in need of renovation, but retaining touches of Victorian charm.

This is a unique, historical alternative to the luxury hotels in Waikiki. You don't have the beach nearby, but you *can* sample flavors of Hawaii's past. And an intriguing note: the inn's previous owner stashed his life savings somewhere on the property!

OUTRIGGER HOTELS HAWAII,
Various locations
(800) 462-6262
Inexpensive to Unbelievably Expensive

Call for directions and reservations at any of the Outrigger properties.

You can't mention hotel kissing on Hawaii without commenting on the Outrigger hotels. This well-known island chain has 27 hotels scattered throughout the four main islands, 22 of them on Oahu. Yet once you've seen the first one, you might as well have seen them all. Outriggers offer relief from Waikiki's otherwise outrageous prices, providing standard hotel accommodations, good service, and sometimes even ocean views for relatively reasonable prices. Generally well-kept and conveniently lo-

cated, Outrigger hotels are ideal for tourists who want to enjoy
Waikiki but don't want to spend a lot of money for luxury. But
don't expect much besides large tour groups coming and going.

ROYAL HAWAIIAN HOTEL, Waikiki   ◆●◀
2259 Kalakaua Avenue
(808) 923-7311, (800) 325-3535
Expensive to Unbelievably Expensive

*Heading east on Kalakaua Avenue, pass the Royal Hawaiian Shopping
Center and the hotel is on the right.*

It's hard to miss this one as you drive down Kalakaua Avenue.
The only precise descriptive words I can think of are *very pink!* The
formidable, colorful exterior dates back to 1927 and has endured
the decades with glamour and panache. You can virtually feel the
history as you walk through the lobby and pathways. Your only
mistake in booking a stay here would be if you are misled into
thinking that the newly built oceanfront tower has the better
accommodations. All of the 192 units located in the Royal Tower,
even the suites, have mediocre furnishings and rather small rooms;
they indeed have great views, but that's it. View would be the *only*
reason to consider these for a romantic romp. All the luxury and
style are in the lovingly renovated rooms in the original main
building. Here you will find high ceilings, generous space, lush
fabrics, unique moldings and trim, attractive baths, and interesting
furnishings. Unfortunately, none of the rooms have views, but the
comfort, size, and history more than compensate for the lack of
ocean air.

There aren't many restaurants or bars that sit directly on the
beach at Waikiki, but the Royal Hawaiian boasts two: the **SURF
ROOM** and the **MAI TAI BAR** (Moderate). The Surf Room can
get crowded and the food is only just OK, but the expanse of beach
is lovely and the Sunday brunch lively and pleasant. The Mai Tai
Bar has a ringside view of the water and is a wonderful casual setting
for sipping cocktails as the day dramatically ebbs into night.

◆ **Romantic Note:** The pool area is unusually small for a hotel
this size and can get beyond crowded to near bursting.

SHERATON MOANA SURFRIDER, Waikiki
2365 Kalakaua Avenue
(808) 922-3111, (800) 325-3535
Expensive to Very Expensive

Heading east on Kalalaua Avenue, pass the Royal Hawaiian Shopping Center and the hotel is on the right. Enter on the second driveway.

Since 1901 the Moana has been a prominent feature in the heart of Waikiki. To some degree, this Sheraton property has remained true to the refined history of its grand hotel building. Outside, an august white plantation-style home with white columns is the center of the complex. Inside, crystal chandeliers, Oriental rugs, extravagant tropical bouquets, sumptuous woods, and elegant, winding staircases fill the lobby, halls, and restaurants. Particularly notable are the **BANYAN VERANDA** (reviewed elsewhere in this section) and **SHIP'S TAVERN** restaurants. The Ship's Tavern has a standard formal setting for dinner with a glass-enclosed view of sultry ocean sunsets and twinkling city lights. The unembellished, ultra-expensive menu serves impressive basic fish and meat dishes, but at these prices they should really be ultra-impressive.

Sadly, once entirely quaint and intimate, the Moana is now mostly a Sheraton, and the two modern wings attached to the old bring the room total to well over 700. However, the renovated wings of the original building are still exceptional, with high ceilings, marble baths, and attractive antique furnishings. Any of these are worth your affectionate consideration. The newer sections need a lot of work (in spite of a recent renovation) to become more than just hotel rooms offering little to no charm or personality.

WAIKIKI JOY HOTEL, Waikiki
320 Lewers Street
(808) 923-2300, (800) 733-5569
Inexpensive to Moderate

Heading east on Kalakaua Avenue, turn left onto Lewers Street; the hotel is on the left.

Inexpensive is hard to come by in Waikiki unless you plan to settle for little more than a hole in the wall with a bed and a window. Unfortunately, reasonable prices can mean just that (and even worse). In our search for economical luxury, we stumbled gratefully over the threshold of this affordable find. The modest though attractive open-air Italian marble lobby is accented by stately white pillars and a small waterfall pond. The tiny swimming pool awkwardly located next to the lobby offers little to no privacy, but unless a swimming pool is essential to your idea of escaping the heat, you won't mind once you've seen the upstairs rooms, which all feature large Jacuzzi soak tubs. The suites themselves are nothing extravagant, but nicely appointed with wicker furnishings and neutral color schemes; some include full kitchens and wet bars. You'll definitely miss the beach, because the views from the lanais are primarily of neighboring rooftops. But considering the price (and the lack of competition at this price range) the Waikiki Joy is a real romantic discovery.

WAIKIKI PARC HOTEL, Waikiki
2233 Helumoa Road
(808) 921-7272, (800) 422-0450
Moderate to Very Expensive

Heading east on Kalakaua Avenue, turn right onto Lewers Street, then right again onto Helumoa Road. The hotel is on the left.

A kissing cousin to the elegant Halekulani across the street, the Parc has none of its neighbor's superior oceanfront drama and luxury. What it does have is a simple lobby, above-average hotel restaurants, and polite, efficient service. But wait, there is a reason for the three-lip rating. Upstairs, each of the rooms in this 22-story building is a delightful place to stay. The higher up you go, the better the view (lower floors only look out to buildings and are subject to street noise), but all the rooms are beautifully done with white shutters, blond wood furnishings, blue tiled baths, and balconies. The pool on the eighth floor sits high enough to have a view of the water and for some reason is often yours alone.

◆   **Romantic Note:** Connected to the Waikiki Parc Hotel, for sushi lovers, is **KACHO** (Inexpensive), a petite restaurant, elegantly appointed, serving fresh udon and even fresher sushi.

Restaurant Kissing

BANYAN VERANDA, Waikiki
2365 Kalakaua Avenue,
at the Sheraton Moana Surfrider Hotel
(808) 922-3111
Expensive

Heading east on Kalalaua Avenue, pass the Royal Hawaiian Shopping Center and the hotel is on the right. Enter on the second driveway.

A white banister encloses this idyllic wraparound terrace restaurant fronting the sapphire blue Pacific. From any angle it is one of the most enticing spots on the island for breakfast, Sunday brunch, or high tea. High-backed wicker chairs, teak floors, and open-air seating create an authentic island setting, while a harpist enhances the mood as light winds blow through the venerable banyan tree in the courtyard. White glove service from a polite staff can be gracious but a little on the haughty side. If you don't mind the formality, you will find romance overflows from this picturesque setting.

CAPPUCCINOS, Waikiki
320 Lewers Street, at the Waikiki Joy Hotel
(808) 923-2300
Inexpensive to Moderate

Heading east on Kalakaua Avenue, turn left onto Lewers Street; the hotel is on the left.

You'd absolutely never expect to find a café with charm and character in Waikiki's drab city streets, but this little corner area is full of pleasant surprises. Cappuccinos greets you with tasteful elegance, marked by Oriental rugs, blond wood furniture, cozy booths, and mint green linens. A faux marble balcony holds several tables perfect for two. Enjoy the ambience and sip a latte or cappuccino done Italian-style. Those with appetites can sample grilled chicken breast, island curry stew, or tofu salad from a limited but very affordable menu. What a perfect place to rejuvenate as you explore the less touristy parts of Waikiki.

HANOHANO ROOM, Waikiki   👄
2255 Kalakaua Avenue, at the Sheraton Waikiki
(808) 922-4422
Very Expensive

In the center of Waikiki, next to the Royal Hawaiian Shopping Center.

The view is the calling card here, which is the major, if not only, reason to include this established restaurant. Ensconced on the 30th floor of the Sheraton, you can dine amidst vast majestic views of the ocean, mountains, and endless sky. Prices are fairly astronomical in light of the kitchen's failings, and there is nothing distinctive or interesting about the interior. Yet there is that view.

Cocktails and snacks are served in their small bar area, which has fine access to the view and a piano player who gently plays into the night. Sunset can be quite an experience from up here if you don't eat.

◆ **Romantic Note: CIAO! AN ITALIAN RESTAURANT,** also at the Sheraton Waikiki, (808) 922-4422, (Moderate), is a true surprise. The attractive interior is softly elegant, with an upscale emphasis that is refined without being artificial or stuffy. Surprisingly well-prepared pastas and pizzas are served in a bright, relaxed setting. You have to make your way through the hordes of guests to get to this one, but it is worth the effort.

◆ **Romantic Warning:** The **Sheraton Waikiki** offers more than 2,000 rooms, so you won't find anything in the accommodations resembling intimacy or charm. In essence, this is really just another of the large developments in Hawaii that capitalize on utilization of space to the exclusion of all else. Nevertheless, some of the suites on the top floor are undergoing much-needed renovation and are actually quite large and comfortable, but that's about the best that can be said.

LA MER, Waikiki
2199 Kalia Road, at the Halekulani Hotel
(808) 923-2311
Expensive to Very Expensive

From Kalakaua Avenue, turn toward the water onto Lewers Street. The hotel will be directly in front of you.

Housed on the second floor of the original private beachfront estate at Halekulani, this dining room is characterized by etched wall panelings and delicious ocean views. Fresh ocean air (and, unfortunately, the sound of next-door evening entertainment) spills into the dining room. Tables cloaked in white linens and garnished with candles enhance the otherwise unadorned and somber surroundings. Island rock fish soup with nohu medallions or grilled sea scallops with kahuku prawns and seafood risotto are among the delectable Pacific Rim selections. You're likely to cast your vote along with others who have rated La Mer's cuisine some of the finest in Oahu.

◆ **Romantic Note:** Although entrées can be absurdly expensive, the three available prix fixe dinners here are a more affordable way to taste a little bit of everything.

◆ **Romantic Alternative:** In order to admire views of Halekulani's grounds and the ocean (and people passing by on the boardwalk) in a more casual climate, you can gaze and graze at the hotel's **HOUSE WITHOUT A KEY,** (808) 923-2311, (Inexpensive to Moderate). The poolside terrace dining room serves a small but eclectic assortment of ethnic cuisine. Simple combinations or a delicious chicken fajita salad are relatively reasonable, and the service is sheer perfection.

KEO'S, Waikiki
1486 South King Street
(808) 947-9988
Inexpensive to Moderate

Call for directions.

Every imaginable celebrity has eaten here, and then some. The proof is on the wall. Peruse the gallery of pictures and see how many stars *you* recognize. This is definitely Waikiki's to-be-seen-in hot spot, and if you eat here you're likely to see at least one famous person—even if you don't recognize them. If you don't care about who's who, come anyway, just to experience the intriguing surroundings and out-of-this-world Thai cuisine.

The noisy dining room is bursting with exotic floral arrangements and abundant greenery, and colorful paintings of flowers and landscapes add to the lush (and crowded) surroundings. Tables nestled snugly throughout the dining room are shaded by umbrellas overhead and separated by white partitions to enhance privacy. You won't mind the tight squeeze once you've tasted the food. Delight in creatively prepared Thai entrées unique to Keo's, such as crispy fried noodles, roll-your-own spring rolls, or their unique Evil Gumbo. Don't forget to order a sweet Thai iced tea—your kisses will taste sweeter than ever.

NICK'S FISHMARKET, Waikiki
2070 Kalakaua Avenue, at the Waikiki Gateway Hotel
(808) 955-6333
Expensive

On Kalakaua Avenue between Kuamoo and Olohana streets.

A tad old-fashioned and a bit too dark for some appetites, Nick's has been serving great fresh fish in Waikiki for as long as anyone can remember. A series of small, intimate dining rooms are interconnected by a tight passageway; the handful of tables in each are set with white tablecloths and fine china. Service is professional (although stuffy) and the food quite good. Large portions of Hawaiian fish are presented in a variety of remarkably tasty sauces. The Chinese black bean sauce and the Thai peanut sauce with grilled eggplant were wonderful.

ORCHIDS, Waikiki
2199 Kalia Road, at the Halekulani Hotel
(808) 923-2311
Moderate to Expensive

From Kalakaua Avenue, turn toward the water onto Lewers Street. The hotel will be directly in front of you.

The Halekulani does everything to perfection. Well, almost. Orchids would be an exemplary spot for romantic dining if it weren't for the nearby boardwalk that inhibits your otherwise ideal ocean views. Provocative floral arrangements and white linens surround you as you dine in the open-air oceanfront dining room, graced by original eucalyptus hardwood floors. You're sure to enjoy the fresh seafood, open ravioli with smoked duck and shiitake mushrooms, or lightly smoked pink snapper steamed in ti leaf with a papaya and Maui onion relish.

REX'S BLACK ORCHID, Waikiki
500 Ala Moana Boulevard
(808) 521-3111
Moderate to Expensive (for dinner)
$10 cover charge if you are only going for the disco

Call for directions.

We discussed this one for a while, whether or not to include it. After all, there isn't much romance to be found in a disco, even one as elegant and slick as this one is. However, if you are in the mood for a more local scene, or just want to shake it loose after a languid day in the sun, Rex's Black Orchid can provide a different kind of upbeat heat.

◆ **Romantic Note:** Although the restaurant can be a bit intense and filled to overflowing, the food is actually quite good and the setting rather sexy. The contemporary Italian menu of pastas, fish, and meat can be tantalizing. The roasted duck in a sun-dried cherry sauce with onion confite is excellent.

THE SECRET, Waikiki
2552 Kalakaua Avenue, at the Hawaiian Regent Hotel
(808) 922-6611
Moderate to Expensive

On Kalakaua Avenue between Ohua and Paokalani avenues.

In Waikiki, your search for reasonably priced, savory Pacific Rim cuisine in intimate surroundings might start to feel futile. Great cooking is not the hallmark of any of the Hawaiian Islands. But don't give up. The Secret offers everything you could ever want and more. In fact, the cuisine and ambience might tempt you to come back again and again (and maybe again).

For a romantic prelude, start out with a cocktail in the softly lit library lounge. Cozy leather couches beckon to couples, and on Thursday, Friday, and Saturday nights you can relax to the strummings of a live classical guitarist.

Standing chandelier torches cast an affectionate glow over a unique dining room that features a high arched-beam ceiling punctuated by colorful Scandinavian flags. Beautiful high-backed wicker chairs lend privacy to snug tables adorned with linens and candlelight. Sensual melodies drift through the room from the grand piano in the corner, enhancing the already amorous mood. Nicely prepared appetizers, such as smoked Norwegian salmon carved tableside and accompanied with capers, onions, shredded eggs, and melba toast, or crab bisque with a touch of brandy, are quite good. Entrées are similarly unusual and tasty, including medallions of veal with essence of truffle on a bed of red, yellow, and green bell peppers topped with macadamia nuts, or French lamb chops with ohelo berry sauce and sun-dried tomatoes, garnished with broiled eggplant. You'll savor every moment of this delicious secret, but try not to tell anyone else.

Diamond Head

Hotel/Bed and Breakfast Kissing

COLONY SURF HOTEL, Diamond Head
2895 Kalakaua Avenue
(808) 923-5751, (800) 252-7873
Moderate to Expensive

Follow Kalakaua Avenue through Waikiki, past Kapiolani Park. Turn right into the parking lot when you see signs for the New Otani Hotel. The Colony Surf is next-door.

Go ahead—close your eyes. The chances of accidently kissing a stranger on the beach are much slimmer here. Diamond Head summons you away from the crowds and mayhem of urban Waikiki, and you follow willingly. (Who wouldn't?) The Colony Surf is one of several desirable yet moderately priced hotels harbored on this tiny stretch of Waikiki Beach, at the foot of Diamond Head and next to a residential park. Waikiki's city skyline stretches on the horizon, a mere ten-minute stroll from the Colony Surf. But the crowds thin out considerably here, leaving somewhat more room for you to relish the surf, sand, and sunshine.

Outside appearances may be discouraging. The Colony Surf's two towers are timeworn and separated by an unattractive parking lot. The only room worth renting in the second tower, which fronts the parking lot, is the exclusive (very expensive) penthouse suite, which is spacious and graced with modern, luxurious decor and a full wraparound view lanai. Yet, even this suite is somewhat weathered, most noticeably in the corners.

Have patience, because more awaits you in the main tower. Your apprehensions will wane once you are sheltered in a sparkling white and pastel one-bedroom suite, awash in sunlight and accented by white wicker furnishings. Enjoy the convenience of a fully equipped (although dated) kitchen and small, standard private bath. Views of Diamond Head or the ocean are yours from the vantage point of a window seat (instead of a lanai) set beneath sizable bay windows that run the width of the room. Sunsets here are truly remarkable. Open the shutters and allow the sound of the gentle surf below and the refreshment of a warm ocean breeze to sweep through the room. What a perfect way to enjoy Waikiki—from a distance.

◆ **Romantic Note:** There's no air conditioning here. Also, the Colony Surf is part hotel and part condominium, so there is an interesting blend of guests and services.

KAHALA BED AND BREAKFAST,
Diamond Head
(808) 885-4550, (800) 262-9912
Inexpensive

Call for directions and reservations.

Ah, sweet mystery of life at last I've found you. The mystery is the lack of professionally run bed and breakfasts on most of the Hawaiian Islands, but particularly Oahu. The find is this luxurious designer mansion turned into an unbelievably wondrous place to stay. While everyone is piled on top of each other in Waikiki, you can savor spacious, luxurious guest suites (they're huge: 2,000 square feet!) for extraordinarily inexpensive prices (we don't know how long this will last), nestled in an exclusive neighborhood. Past the security gate you enter a large brick courtyard filled with plants and a tiled swimming pool. Each room has its own private entrance and all are a sight to behold. Antique furnishings abound along with a private deck overlooking the canal and 18th hole of a championship golf course. A well-stocked kitchen, large splendid bedroom, bath, and living room are all yours. Believe us, this one will be hard to leave.

KAHALA HILTON, Diamond Head
5000 Kahala Avenue
(808) 734-2211, (800) HILTONS
Moderate to Expensive

Call for directions.

Unmarred stretches of sandy beach, the verdant rolling hills of the surrounding Waialae Country Club Golf Course, and clusters of palm trees enfold this luxury oceanfront resort in hushed seclusion, seducing romantics of all kinds. Once you've tasted the privacy here, it's hard to imagine anybody would choose to go elsewhere. However, our enthusiasm for the Kahala Hilton is not because of the decor. The interior is quite dated and has a stuffy country-club ambience. Still, you can almost glimpse paradise in its original splendor here, the natural tropical beauty seemingly untouched by Waikiki's overactive development.

The Kahala Hilton's 369 rooms, a relatively small number for a Hawaiian resort, are spacious and comfortable. Most have commodious private lanais with breathtaking unmarred, expansive ocean views. The bathrooms have private his-and-her dressing areas and a separate tub and shower. Decor is simple and understated (and also in need of renovation), but it's still pleasant.

You can leave Waikiki behind you for the duration of your stay because the hotel provides most major hotel conveniences, such as gourmet restaurants (very expensive, even for breakfast), music and dancing in the Maile Lounge (one of our favorites in all of Oahu), gift shops, art galleries, beauty salon, car rental and travel desk, florist, jewelers, and even a newsstand. The **MAILE** (reviewed elsewhere in this section), one of our favorite restaurants on Oahu, is also located here. So settle in; there's no need to go anywhere but the beach.

Romantic potential blossoms on the landscaped oceanfront grounds. The water is your playground, and kayaks, rafts, paddleboats, and snorkeling equipment are available for guests' use. Walking paths meander past a swimming pool, a tumbling waterfall, and a man-made lagoon that is home to several exotic animals, including turtles, penguins, and bottlenosed dolphins (who perform for guests three times daily and are partial to guests' baseball hats). One path continues past the seemingly deserted beach and out onto a tiny peninsula dotted with park benches perfect for long embraces and lingering sunsets.

◆   **Romantic Note:** The **MAUNALUA BAY CLUB**, a two-acre, oceanfront tennis club and fitness center, is available to guests (for an extra charge of $15 a day) and accessible via a complimentary shuttle bus. Amenities include six night-lighted tennis courts ($20 an hour), saunas, Nautilus equipment, aerobic classes, a Jacuzzi, a snack bar, and a swimming pool.

◆   **Romantic Warning:** Traditions at the Kahala Hilton die hard. The 20-year continuing dinner entertainment here is provided by Danny Kaleikini and his Polynesian Revue, performing hula, fire dancing, and Hawaiian songs (six nights a week) in the downstairs Hala Terrace. It's more noisy than enjoyable for those not in attendance, and can be intrusive if you leave your lanai door open at night.

NEW OTANI KAIMANA BEACH HOTEL,
Diamond Head
2863 Kalakaua Avenue
(808) 923-1555, (800) 733-7949
Inexpensive to Unbelievably Expensive

Follow Kalakaua Avenue into Diamond Head and watch for signs to the hotel on the right.

Almost everything about the New Otani Hotel is worth praising. Located right on the narrow stretch of Kaimana Beach, the ivory sands and blue water are less crowded here than in Waikiki. A small but appealing open-air lobby is decorated in a gracious Oriental motif that continues through the rest of the 125 guest rooms. Newly refurbished rooms are exceedingly desirable and spacious. Private balconies, large floor-to-ceiling windows, and pastel fabrics and wall coverings create an inviting atmosphere. Many of the rooms have impressive views of the glorious water, with downtown Waikiki in the distance. Of particular romantic interest are the large, beautifully designed suites on the upper floors. Sensually furnished and uniquely appointed, they leave little doubt that the extra expense (minimal in comparison to other hotels in the area) is something your lips will appreciate.

From the least expensive to the most expensive, each room has the makings for a blissful getaway. That alone rates the New Otani as a rare find on any of the islands, but especially Oahu.

◆   **Romantic Warning:** The New Otani is pigeonholed in a row of low-rise condominium buildings. Although inside you may not notice, outside it is hard to avoid the congestion. It isn't as bad as Waikiki, but it isn't paradise either.

Restaurant Kissing

HAU TREE LANAI, Diamond Head
2863 Kalakaua Avenue, at the New Otani Kaimana Beach Hotel
(808) 923-1555
Moderate

Follow Kalakaua Avenue into Diamond Head and watch for signs to the hotel and restaurant on the right.

Share sunset on a lovely open-air terrace beneath a spreading hau tree, just off the beach, overlooking the water. Ocean breezes drift past cozy tables covered with white tablecloths, set under pink umbrellas. You're sure to appreciate the chef's prize-winning cuisine, such as sautéed Hawaiian nairagi (striped marlin) covered with green onion and a Malaysian curry sauce or fresh mango chutney. Any time of day you will find this a quaint, ambrosial place for holding hands and dining.

MAILE RESTAURANT and LOUNGE, ◆◆◆
Diamond Head
5000 Kahala Avenue, at the Kahala Hilton
(808) 734-2211
Expensive to Very Expensive

Call for directions.

Let me tell you about the things that make this place so enticingly romantic. The service is the personification of island warmth, the dinner music of light piano is dreamy, and the room is perfectly lit for intimacy (but not for looking out the windows, because there aren't any). Of essential amorous interest is the exceptionally talented four-piece band performing Tuesday through Saturday nights, playing soft jazz and Latin music for arm-in-arm two-stepping. Each musician sings, and does so beautifully.

What makes Maile somewhat less than romantic is outdated decor that is a bit on the stuffy side. Their classic continental menu is somewhat lackluster (the same entrées as most of the other hotel restaurants in town), but unlike many other choice restaurants, these dishes are well executed and delicious. The crowd is the generation that revels in sambas and waltzes, not a negative, but depending on your point of view you may feel out of place. To our way of thinking (or embracing), it is a superb kissing place.

MICHEL'S, Diamond Head
2895 Kalakaua Avenue, at the Colony Surf Hotel
(808) 923-6552
Expensive

Follow Kalakaua Avenue through Waikiki, past Kapiolani Park. Turn right into the parking lot when you see signs for the New Otani Hotel. The Colony Surf is next-door.

I don't often agree with the television show *Lifestyles of the Rich and Famous*; after all, the rich and famous are often too concerned with pretense and power to be interested in kissing. Plus, I've never heard a critical comment from the commentator, and most of the places he recommends are not as perfect as he would have you believe. Such is true for Michel's.

The ambience here is unquestionably sensual. In fact, it would be hard to find more amorous surroundings. The plush open-air dining room is nestled directly on the beach and offers panoramic views of the ocean surf and Waikiki beyond. The three connecting dining rooms exude elegance at every turn. Cozy, candlelit tables for two are draped in white linens, adorned with hand-painted plates, and set beneath overhanging, dimly lit crystal chandeliers and gilded mirrors. The menu features some excellent culinary feats including seared peppersteak flamed in whiskey and black peppercorn sauce, and delicate coho salmon garnished with shrimp and served in a beurre blanc sauce, but the desserts were disenchanting, as were the appetizers. The menu is not nearly as innovative as we had hoped it would be (especially at these prices), and the service was awkward and disappointing. Breakfast is probably the most romantic time to be here, and the kitchen doesn't disappoint then. Lunch on a summer day would be perfect, but the sunbathers beyond the rail are distracting and less than picturesque.

Kailua

Hotel/Bed and Breakfast Kissing

MANU MELE BED AND BREAKFAST, Kailua   ◆◆
153 Kailuana Place
(808) 262-0016
Inexpensive

Call for directions.

A residential area about 20 minutes east of Waikiki is the congenial location for this immaculate, handsomely renovated bed and breakfast. All three guest rooms are attractively furnished and have sliding glass doors that open to the pool and a well-tended garden courtyard. Each room has a microwave, coffee maker, refrigerator, and television. A nearby path leads to a sweeping, fairly empty stretch of sun-kissed sand at Kailua Bay. The only drawback to this kissing bargain is the adjacent thoroughfare. Cars whiz by and the sound is less than idyllic, but the price, nearby beach, and the owners' attention to detail more than make up for this urban drawback.

> *"...once he drew*
> *With one long kiss my whole soul thro'*
> *My lips, as sunlight drinketh dew."*
> Alfred, Lord Tennyson

Maui

> *"What of soul was left,*
> *I wonder, when the kissing*
> *had to stop?"*
>
> Robert Browning

MAUI

All of the idyllic words used to describe practically anyone's concept of paradise are associated with this wondrous corner of heaven. Surely the garden of Eden looked something like Maui, well, at least the Maui of 20 years ago. Unfortunately, Maui's glory is no longer a secret, and the resulting popularity and growth have left their mark. The scenery here is as often dotted by condominium developments as it is by lush tropical forests, azure waters, and pristine beaches. Cars cover the handful of main roads that circle the island, creating slow-moving traffic jams. But they're not *really* traffic jams, not if you change your focus and concentrate on the scenery and warm air. Then everything is forgivable.

Besides being the second-largest island in the Hawaiian chain, Maui is also considered the island of the well-heeled. There are more millionaires per capita here than anywhere else in the U.S. The most expensive hotel rooms in the world are located here on Maui: two suites at the Grand Hyatt in Wailea that go for $8,500 a night. I won't describe what you get for that: it would only cause you a great deal of envy and potential kissing distress. Although there are a preponderance of costly properties that are stupendous places to stay, there are also less prohibitive spots that can feel almost as indulgent and grand.

For those of you who have never visited Maui (and even for those who come again and again), certain tourist activities (requiring only a car and the appropriate gear) are mandatory on any romantic (or nonromantic) itinerary: witnessing sunrise or sunset on top of **HALEAKALA CRATER**; hiking **IAO VALLEY STATE PARK** to discover the 2,250-foot rocky spire of **IAO NEEDLE**; driving two and a half hours through lush tropical rain forest, navigating more than 600 hairpin turns, to the remote scenic town of **HANA** and the dramatic **SEVEN POOLS** waterfall just outside of Kipahulu; snorkeling off **BLACK ROCK** in Kaanapali; strolling through the old whaling village of **LAHAINA**;

watching the surfers hang ten at **HOOKIPA PARK** on the north side of the island; and enjoying a leisurely Sunday brunch at any of the half dozen or so prodigious hotel developments that hug exquisite sections of the island and treat you like royalty. All of this is the well-known and extremely impressive side of Maui, and, for the most part (except for brunch), it is all free.

Those who have a larger vacation budget can bicycle down Haleakala on an organized biking trek (about $100 per person); helicopter to Hana or just take a helicopter sight-seeing ride (about $95 and up per person); go on a wide variety of boat rides out to the extinct crater of Molokini or other less public snorkeling spots (about $65 to $95 per person); take scuba diving lessons (rates vary widely, but can cost up to $150 for three hours); or have a premium gourmet dinner at any of the aforementioned Disneyesque hotels (about $100 to $150 for two).

Finding the romance in all this has to do more with your budget, the time of year, and the time of day you venture out. All of the paid-for activities are well organized, fun, and can take you to extraordinary places. If you have to choose only one, we suggest a catarman ride that includes snorkeling or an evening sunset sail (reviewed in the Honolua Bay entry). For information on all of these activities, call the Maui tourist office at (808) 871-8691.

The rest of the listings here will help you indulge your romantic inclinations on the less touristy, more intimate parts of your trip.

◆ **Romantic Warning:** You will hear quite a lot about the beauty of witnessing sunrise on the top of Haleakala (at 10,000 feet it is spectacular), but so has everyone else on the island (including those who are part of the downhill bicycle excursions). The line of buses and cars on this windy, fog-shrouded road at 4:00 a.m. in the morning is nothing less than astonishing. And it is cold up here at sunrise; expect (and prepare for) 30-degree temperatures. It does warm up later in the day so wear layers of clothing that you can shed as the sun heats the mountain air. It is definitely worth a drive up to see this extinct volcanic crater, but there are other, less crowded times than first thing in the morning. Sunset is just as beautiful, and the weather is more apt to be clear and the traffic jams almost (remember, we said almost) nonexistent. For more information, call Haleakala National Park, (808) 572-9177.

Equally popular are the snorkeling cruises to the extinct volcanic crater of Molokini. The trip out is wonderful, but the crescent-shaped rocky rim can be like a parking lot for boats, it is that popular. In fact, the fish are so overfed here they often appear nonchalant about your food offerings. There are more secluded spots for snorkeling that are just as beautiful, and those are the ones we've included.

◆ **Romantic Historical Note:** Maui is the name of the god who created all the Hawaiian Islands. The story goes something like this: At the beginning of time Maui used his legendary rope to hook the land submerged under the seas to form the islands. After accomplishing this mythic feat, Maui then attempted to lasso the sun god, La, to bring light to the islands. Their great struggle took place at the top of Haleakala. Maui emerged victorious. In a dire effort to obtain his freedom, the enslaved La promised to travel slowly across the heavens to forever warm the people and their harvests. It is for these benevolent acts that the god Maui came to have an island named after him.

Kapalua

Quite literally the end of the road for the westernmost tip of Maui, Kapalua is one of the least developed places on the island (and it is likely to stay that way). Although you wouldn't exactly call this place remote, the traffic and crowds thin out immensely up here. Depending on your preferences, there are many things that can make this a desirable area and a few things that might make it disappointing. The West Maui mountains, 23,000 acres of pineapple fields, and a rugged shoreline define this lush, majestic realm. Because of the location it is also the wettest area of the island. That might mean a few more clouds and an extra hour or two of precipitation during the rainy season, but that's about it. Among Kapalua's virtues are its truly remote, unmarked beaches (all but three are a bit of a hike to get to), ideal for playing in the surf; an incredibly scenic drive (somewhat inaccessible without a four-wheel-drive vehicle) from Honokahua to Kahakuloa; and a welcome feeling of relative seclusion. The area isn't isolated, but in comparison to other sections of Maui it is secluded and private.

Hotel/Bed and Breakfast Kissing

PINEAPPLE HILL HOMES, Kapalua ◆◆◆◆
500 Office Road
(808) 669-8088, (800) 545-0018
Unbelievably Expensive ($700 to $800 a day)

Call for directions.

High atop the scintillating Kapalua coastline, snuggle in the lap of luxury at this stunning development of grand designer homes. There is plenty of room between the properties, guaranteeing supreme privacy. Each house has its own tile swimming pool or large outdoor Jacuzzi tub, electric garage, designer kitchen and bathroom, sumptuous furnishings, and sensational views. Yes, the price tag is steep, but you are buying a once-in-a-lifetime getaway filled with splendid romantic opportunity.

RITZ-CARLTON, Kapalua ◆◆◆◆
One Ritz-Carlton Way
(808) 669-6200, (800) 262-8440
Unbelievably Expensive and Beyond

From Highway 30, turn west at the Kapalua marker and follow the signs to the hotel.

Beaches and sunshine are to Hawaii what service and understated elegance are to the Ritz-Carlton: quintessential givens that reward visitors with a superlative vacation experience. A stay at the Ritz will leave you feeling utterly pampered and regal. The attention to detail here is astounding. Your every whim is almost magically attended to. A glass of water appears poolside even before you can ask for it; no fewer than three towels are arranged properly on your pool- or oceanside chair; iced Evian water is available at the entry to the hotel every morning for joggers; and turndown service includes a thorough recleaning of your room. European refinement (a Ritz trademark) is evident in the formal fabrics and gilt-edged furnishings and appointments. The rooms, mostly upscale hotel-basic with large marble bathrooms and small but adequate lanais with wrought-iron furniture, are less impressive than the setting. Most have a decent to sublime view of the water, and the rest look out to the emerald Maui mountains.

Like many of the fabulous hotel properties on Maui, the Ritz offers amenities such as a variety of outstanding restaurants, a gorgeous pool area, and a spectacular sandy beach. As amazing as it seems, all of the restaurants here receive unusually high praise. One of the absolute best on the island is **THE GRILL** (reviewed elsewhere in this section). For a more casual repast, try **THE BEACH HOUSE** or **THE BANYAN TREE**. The Beach House serves a small casual menu of sandwiches and salads along with a full bar. It is splendidly located directly on Old Fleming Beach with comfortable white tables and chairs set on the edge of a sandy bluff, out in the open. It is an absolutely perfect setting for a delightful break in your bathing suit. The Banyan Tree (reviewed elsewhere in this section) has the same glorious views, even though the setting is elegant, poolside casual.

◆   **Romantic Alternative:** In its heyday about 15 years ago, the **KAPALUA BAY HOTEL**, One Bay Drive, Kapalua, (808) 669-5656, (800) 367-8000, (Unbelievably Expensive), was a sight to behold. Its massive open lobby, spectacular oceanfront location, and truly ample rooms with large, sensual marble baths made it a rare phenomenon along these shores. Now the property is in pressing need of renovation, and a new owner is being sought to put much-needed money into the project. Its glory days may be a thing of the past, but the prices are right up there with the new premier island properties. The hotel also offers two great restaurants(the **PLANTATION VERANDA** and the **BAY CLUB**, both reviewed elsewhere in this section), and a nearby beach once rated the best on theisland. The service is less than what you would expect at these rates.

◆   **Second Romantic Alternative: BAY VILLA CONDO-MINIUMS**, 129 Bay Drive, Kapalua, (808) 669-0210, (800) 545-VIEW, (Unbelievably Expensive), offers beautifully appointed uits with tall ceilings, set on or near the rocky shore of the ocean. Too bad they aren't air-conditioned; even the trade winds can't cool off a hot day.

Restaurant Kissing

THE BANYAN TREE   ◆◆◆◆
RESTAURANT, Kapalua
One Ritz-Carlton Way, in the Ritz-Carlton
(808) 669-6200, (800) 262-8440
Moderate

From Highway 30, turn west at the Kapalua marker and follow the signs to the hotel.

This casual oceanfront dining spot serves Italian fare that is simply sensational. The entire restaurant is open air, and the wicker chairs, marble-topped wrought-iron tables, and large tiled floor give it the air of an elegant bistro. The view out to the ocean and mountains makes up for proximity to the mostly sedate crowd gathered around the nearby pool. Tempting entrées include the spicy lamb and spinach cannelloni with a delicious goat cheese and pepper sauce, and pizza topped with duck sausage, sun-dried tomatoes, roasted garlic, and cilantro. In the early evening, between 5:00 and 7:00, the restaurant serves only platters of pupus (Hawaiian for "appetizers") and cocktails.

THE BAY CLUB, Kapalua   ◆◆◆
One Bay Drive, adjacent to the Kapalua Bay Hotel
(808) 669-5656
Very Expensive

From Highway 30, take the Kapalua exit and follow the signs for the Kapalua Bay Hotel. The restaurant is adjacent to the hotel.

The sound of the surf accompanies your leisurely meal at this handsome open-air restaurant situated on a small bluff just above the water's edge. Linger over creatively prepared fish dishes at lunch or dinner, then contemplate the vast ocean from the nearby beach.

THE GRILL RESTAURANT, Kapalua
One Ritz-Carlton Way, in the Ritz-Carlton
(808) 669-6200, (800) 262-8440
Expensive to Unbelievably Expensive

From Highway 30, turn west at the Kapalua marker and follow the signs to the hotel.

This bastion of exquisite dining deserves a less understated name. The service is flawless, the formal setting simply stunning, and the food the most tantalizing and brilliantly presented on the island. There is little to inhibit a leisurely romantic evening. Begin your night out in the stately lounge adjacent to the restaurant, where handsome love seats and plush armchairs invite you to snuggle close while you listen to light jazz performed by a pianist and singer. Once you are seated for dinner, the menu works its own seduction. Don't even try to resist the Molokai sweet potato lasagne with shiitake cream sauce, silky smooth seafood chowder, or roasted salmon encrusted in spinach and potato with an anise sauce. Every dessert is a masterpiece, and the sweet sensations are sheer ecstasy.

PINEAPPLE HILL RESTAURANT, Kapalua
500 Office Road
(808) 669-6129
Expensive

Turn right off Highway 30 at the sign for Kapalua and follow the signs to the restaurant.

The Pineapple Hill Restaurant may be a bit boring for some tastes, but the food can be quite good and the view at sundown is even better. In winter sunset is too early to coincide with your meal,

but later in the year it lingers on and on and so can your meal. The
exterior and interior are reminiscent of a country home, and the
feeling is relaxed and casual. The cuisine is international with an
emphasis on steak and fresh fish, mostly well prepared, but occa-
sionally inconsistent. Still, the view makes up for everything.

PLANTATION HOUSE RESTAURANT, Kapalua
2000 Plantation Club Drive
(808) 669-6299
Moderate to Expensive

*Take Highway 30 to just north of the Kapalua entrance. On the right
side of the highway, look for the Plantation Golf Course and turn right
up to the restaurant.*

Set high on a hill with a breathtaking view of the water and
surrounding emerald fields and forests, this restaurant is a must for
its vantage point alone. Thank goodness there is more to be found
here. Daily brunch and dinner are both enjoyable at this golf club
dining room, although the ambience is more social and jovial than
romantic (most of the tables are set for larger groups). But the view
and the attractive interior of light wood, high beamed ceilings,
comfortable high-backed chairs, fireplace, and open-to-the-air
windows more then make up for the golfing state of mind. Most of
the entrées are quite good and the fish is served fresh and moist.
Sadly, the salads can be mediocre and the fried calamari tough.
However, at sunset when the sky blazes bright, and during the day
when the air is soft and breezy, everything tastes a little bit better.

PLANTATION VERANDA, Kapalua
One Bay Drive, in the Kapalua Bay Hotel
(808) 669-5656
Expensive

*From Highway 30, take the Kapalua exit and follow the signs for the
Kapalua Bay Hotel. The restaurant is on the lower level of the hotel.*

In spite of the big hotel setting, this brightly colored restaurant
feels amazingly secluded and quaint, with a towering wall of French

doors that open to let the warm breezes caress the interior. It is a lovely setting for a tropical dining experience. The excellent food is decidedly French and beautifully presented. Have a leisurely romantic dinner here, then take a moonlight stroll hand-in-hand along the beach.

Outdoor Kissing

OLD FLEMING BEACH, Kapalua

Access the beach from Highway 30 north of the Ritz Carlton, after you've passed the Kapalua sign.

This is a remarkable stretch of beach, possibly one of the most beautiful in the world. The sand is silky soft and surrounded by rocky outcroppings, with rolling green hills in the distance. Depending on the weather, the surf either rolls lazily in or surges several feet in the air and comes crashing down in a rush of white water.

The Ritz-Carlton's Beach House and Banyan Tree restaurants are close by, so you can enjoy a mai tai, piña colada, or delicious pupus after you've played in the rolling waves.

HONOLUA BAY, Kapalua

Access the beach from Highway 30, about three miles north of Kapalua.

Cars parked on either side of the road are the only obvious marker at this extraordinary snorkeling bay. A short, steep walk through forest brings you to the inviting, relatively secluded rocky beach. Swim alongside colorful tropical fish and, unique to this spot, large sea turtles. It is fascinating to watch these gentle giants swim in and out of their caves.

◆ **Romantic Note:** Two catamarans will capture the breeze in their sails to whisk you here in style. The Hyatt Regency's **KIELE V,** (808) 661-1234, extension 3104, has a tour that goes out, as does the **KAPALUA KAI,** (808) 669-4665. Cost is about $70 per person, and about 40 other eager fish enthusiasts will join you, but the trip is a wonderful opportunity to see the island from out in the water.

DRIVE FROM HONOKAHUA
TO KAHAKULOA

Follow Highway 30 past Kapalua, until the road signs warn you not to go on.

Most rental car companies don't want you traveling this stretch of road generously described as unimproved and unpassable. During the rainy season the road may not exist at all. However, dry days and a four-wheel-drive vehicle can afford you the opportunity to explore the jungle-like northernmost region of Maui. This is *not* a tourist area and there are no facilities or amenities along the way, but the views are remarkable and the local villages are fascinating. If you are here between December and March, keep your eyes open for humpback whales.

Napili

Buried between the high-rent districts of Kapalua and Kaanapali, the town of Napili has a plethora of condominium developments and hotels piled one on top of the other without breathing room or much beachfront. There are some bargains to be found here, but the sacrifice is often air-conditioning and privacy. It isn't my favorite section of Maui, but it is only a stone's throw from its neighbors' nearby remarkable beaches and restaurants. The decision is yours.

HONOKEANA COVE, Napili Bay
5255 Lower Honoapiilani Road
(808) 669-6441
Inexpensive to Moderate

Just north of Kaanapali, turn west off Highway 30 at the Napili turnoff, which becomes Honoapiilani Road.

The Honokeana Cove is a low-rise with only two levels, creating a welcome feeling of ample space and openness. Like many other condominium units along the coast, the rooms here have private lanais, petite fully equipped kitchen areas (including dishwasher), nice-sized living rooms with comfortable furnishings, small, rather lackluster baths, and no air-conditioning. (Laundry facilities are available on-site but not in the units.) The draw is the view out to the water and the island of Molokai in the distance. The pool is set at the edge of a rocky bluff, a relatively secluded cove below has great snorkeling, and, a short walk away, there is a sandy beach with rolling waves to play in. The price is right, and the location is actually quite wonderful.

NAPILI KAI BEACH CLUB, Napili Bay
5900 Honoapiilani Road
(808) 669-6271, (800) 367-5030
Expensive to Unbelievably Expensive

Just north of Kaanapali, turn west off Highway 30 at the Napili turnoff, which becomes Honoapiilani Road.

A large sprawling hotel complex with ten separate buildings fronts a gorgeous stretch of open water and sandy beach. The 162 units vary in size from studios to three-bedroom suites with two baths. Most rooms have immaculate comfortable furnishings that are a bit on the worn side, efficiency kitchens, air-conditioning, shoji screens separating the bedroom from the bath or living room, and sizable lanais. The buildings vary in size, from two to four stories. Privacy is limited because walkways meander in front of many of the rooms. The most desirable (and expensive) units are in Puna Point and Puna 2; these all look out to an obstructed view of the Pacific and have been recently renovated.

Three pools, two tennis courts, a large outdoor whirlpool, and free use of snorkels and fins are all available for guests. There is also a delightful little restaurant called the **SEA HOUSE RESTAU-RANT,** (808) 669-1500, (Moderate), with a premier location on the beach. Open for breakfast, lunch, and dinner, the Sea House serves standard American dishes with little flair but ample portions. Although you might not want to spend an intimate dinner here, this just may be one of the best places on the island for a serenely romantic inexpensive breakfast.

ONE NAPILI WAY, Napili
5355 Lower Honoapiilani Road
(808) 669-2007, (800) 841-6284
Inexpensive to Moderate

Just north of Kaanapali, turn west off Highway 30 at the Napili turnoff,
which becomes Honoapiilani Road.

Sans view but attractively appointed, this unusually small condo
complex has only 14 units, which feature towering wood-beamed
ceilings, comfy cane furniture, nicely sized kitchens with large
refrigerators, attractive baths with a small Jacuzzi tub, television
with VCR, ceiling fans in every room, and plentiful windows.
These bright, roomy rentals are available with one, two, or three
bedrooms. The units front well-tended gardens and swaying palm
trees, and a small but crystal-clear pool with an outdoor spa is set
out back.

◆   **Romantic Note:** This property has minimum-stay requirements for high (five nights) and low season (four nights).

Kaanapali

A few years back the Kaanapali coast was considered the
premium enchantment of Maui. Two miles of soft sandy beach
with gentle rolling waves made it the most desirable of Hawaiian
areas. Unfortunately, the proliferation of high-rise condominiums and mega-resort hotels has changed this once-serene location to a crowded mess. Do not expect calm here, particularly
during high season. All of the properties in this area tout rooms
that are referred to as having a garden or mountain view. You
might very well see beautiful gardens and mountains from these,
and the prices are reasonable, but you will also see (and hear) a
barrage of traffic. The noise can be maddening. (Of course, the
restaurants and ocean-view rooms are free from this offense.)
Please note that all of the Hotel/Bed and Breakfast recommenda-

tions in this area are only in consideration of the location. Even the most beautiful property can become intolerable if a romantic interlude or a dreamy morning in your room is marred by slamming car doors and screeching brakes.

Surprisingly, the beach is still radiant, and because the hotel and condominium properties all have great pool areas, it is relatively uncrowded. For swimming and soaking up the sun, this is a great location. For romance, well, you won't be alone even for a minute.

Hotel/Bed and Breakfast Kissing

EMBASSY SUITES, Kaanapali
104 Kaanapali Shores Place
(808) 661-2000, (800) 462-6284
Expensive to Unbelievably Expensive

At the north end of Kaanapali Beach, just off Highway 30.

This towering pink building has a waterfall tumbling down the middle of its 12 stories. In some ways it is one of the most conspicuous buildings anywhere to be found on Maui, but it is also a charming hotel where every room is a large, beautifully appointed suite. A 35-inch television, VCR, stereo system, a tiny kitchenette with microwave and refrigerator, and a sizable lanai are found in each unit. The bathrooms are surprisingly sensual, with two-person soak tubs and separate glass-enclosed showers all framed in white tile.

In addition to the extra space you also receive a generous cooked-to-order complimentary breakfast buffet and early-evening cocktail hour. The fairly average pool area opens to a sandy beach with tranquil surf. All this, plus the open-air lobby, water views from many rooms, and the reliably good **OHANA GRILL**, directly on the beach, makes the Embassy, to borrow a phrase from the management, one "suite deal." In fact, in comparison to other oceanfront hotels, the prices are downright reasonable.

HYATT REGENCY MAUI, Kaanapali
200 Nohea Kai Drive
(808) 661-1234, (800) 233-1234
Expensive to Unbelievably Expensive

On Kaanapali Beach, just off Highway 30.

Four years ago, when we first visited the Hyatt Regency on Kaanapali Beach, it was an outstanding experience, one we will never forget. The towering building encircles an open courtyard filled with tropical plants and palm trees. A jungle-like pool area with a delightful three-story slide only steps away from the ocean made the Hyatt a fantasy escape unlike any other.

In many ways nothing has changed. What *has* changed is the development of even more spectacular hotel properties that make the Hyatt Regency seem more ordinary. It is still a premium resort, and the restaurants here (particularly the **SWAN COURT**, reviewed elsewhere in this section) are first-class, but the rooms are pretty much nice hotel standard, and they show a little more wear than you would expect. The mountain-view rooms have an equally accessible view of the parking area and busy Highway 30.

◆ **Romantic Note:** The Hyatt has a computer program for couples, called **DISCOVERIES IN ROMANCE,** to help you begin your vacation or spice things up if you are having trouble deciding what to do with all this intimate time alone. We enjoyed it. It created some interesting discussions and gave us some good ideas of where to go on the island.

For $10 each, you can experience the Hyatt's **TOUR OF THE STARS.** On top of the hotel's roof is an elaborately assembled telescope where you can see and learn about the stars. A closer acquaintance with various heavenly bodies could put romantic ideas in your head.

MAUI KAI, Kaanapali
106 Kaanapali Shores Place
(808) 667-3500, (800) 367-5635
Inexpensive to Expensive

On Kaanapali Beach, next door to the Embassy Suites Hotel.

Hugging Kaanapali Beach is this relatively small condominium building of truly charming one-bedroom units. They aren't fancy—in some ways they are rather plain—but they are all oceanfront units with wonderful eight-foot-deep lanais, ample windows, and unparalleled views. Central air-conditioning, comfortable furnishings, a small but attractive pool area with accompanying Jacuzzi, and a sandy beach next door make this a wonderful find on the Kaanapali coast.

◆ **Romantic Note:** A two-night minimum stay is required.

ROYAL LAHAINA RESORT, Kaanapali
2780 Kekaa Drive
(808) 661-3611, (800) 44-ROYAL
Moderate to Unbelievably Expensive

On Kaanapali Beach, just off Highway 30.

A one-lip rating might not seem all that exciting, but the oceanfront rooms here are actually quite lovely and spacious, and probably deserve an extra lip or two. The hotel is located at the north end of Kaanapali Beach, so it's a bit out of the rush of things. Three pools set on different levels help you desalinate after a day of ducking in and out of waves on the wide, sandy beach. Unfortunately, the restaurants here leave much to be desired and the hotel in general could use a great deal of refurbishing. Enjoy the oceanfront rooms (or splurge on one of the oceanfront cottages to feel like you have a home near the surf) and venture into the heart of Kaanapali or Kapalua for your dining pleasures.

SHERATON MAUI HOTEL, Kaanapali
Kaanapali Beach
(808) 661-0031, (800) 325-3535
Moderate to Unbelievably Expensive

On Kaanapali Beach at Black Rock.

I know this might seem hard to believe, but the most inexpensive rooms at the Sheraton Maui are really the most desirable. For the most part this property is incredibly run-down and overrated.

The beach directly in front of the hotel is one of the best around and has great snorkeling, but the decor inside is little better than what you would expect from a budget motel and a musty smell is pervasive throughout. Even the so-called prime rooms overlook the pool area, the roof, and then the ocean in the distance. The oldest section of the hotel, called the Molokai Wing, suffers from many of the same problems as the rest of the hotel (perhaps even more so), but it sits directly atop a rocky shoreline and has an expansive open view of the water. The price is consistent with the quality of the accommodations ($130 a night is a bargain in this neighborhood), but the view is priceless.

The Sheraton's **DISCOVERY ROOM** restaurant is best described as disenchanting, in spite of its remarkable vantage point atop Black Rock. Avoid it and go straight to the hotel's bar, **ON THE ROCKS**. From here the Pacific stretches out before you in all its glory, with the sun setting the sky ablaze or a whale breaching in the distance.

WESTIN MAUI, Kaanapaili   ◆◆
2365 Kaanapali Parkway
(808) 667-2525, (800) 228-3000
Expensive to Unbelievably Expensive

On Kaanapali Beach, just off Highway 30.

If only more of the rooms in the lower priced categories (still in the Unbelievably Expensive range) weren't so disappointing, this would be a remarkable place to stay. The luxury and splendor of the lobby and the hotel's restaurants (the **SOUND OF THE FALLS RESTAURANT** is reviewed elsewhere in this section) are legendary, and they more than live up to their acclaim. An exceptionally delightful multilevel pool area, complete with slides, waterfalls, and grottos, borders the exquisite Kaanapali Beach. Unfortunately, you can't sleep in these gracious common areas. Many of the suites have mountain views that have to contend with a fairly busy parking lot and entryway, something the brochure forgets to mention. Some of the rooms could also stand a bit of sprucing up; most are simply standard hotel rooms. Even many of the rooms with views of the water are set back from the shore and focus on the lobby and pool. The more desirable, most expensive rooms are in the Beach Tower. These are by far the most beautifully appointed, with the best views.

◆ **Romantic Note:** Ask about the Westin's Romance Packages and Wedding Packages. They include everything you can think of, including the minister.

Restaurant Kissing

SOUND OF THE FALLS, Kaanapali
2365 Kaanapali Parkway, in the Westin Maui
(808) 667-2525, (800) 228-3000
Expensive to Unbelievably Expensive

On Kaanapali Beach, just off Highway 30.

Perhaps not as breathtaking as the Swan Court, its romantic neighbor down the road, the Sound of the Falls is still a lovely setting for an open-air dinner or Sunday brunch. Inside, pink flamingos perch on islands of palm trees set in the middle of a striking pond where cascading waterfalls tumble down a rocky embankment into the clear water. Just behind the pond, the ocean's surf accompanies the pianist with a gentle surging rhythm. Coral and black marble floors, napkins, and glasses echo the aforementioned long-necked birds. The cuisine is a blend of continental and California-style dishes and can be quite good, though sometimes inconsistent. The service is very attentive.

SWAN COURT, Kaanapali
200 Nohea Kai Drive, in the Hyatt Regency
(808) 661-1234, (800) 233-1234
Expensive to Unbelievably Expensive

On Kaanapali Beach, just off Highway 30.

It doesn't get much more romantic than this. If only the dinner here lived up to the ambience it would rate ten lips. The atmosphere is luxuriantly sumptuous, and the service exemplary. The towering front wall of open-air windows looks out to a dramatic pond where gracefully poised black and white swans glide by with the ocean in the background, enhancing the elegantly sensuous mood. The grand menu reads like a symphony, but the performance is on the bland side, lacking seasoning and finesse. However, the desserts are perfectly exquisite, particularly the mango soufflé with ginger anglaise crème ladled in the middle.

Like many other hotel restaurants in Hawaii, the Swan Court serves a daily breakfast/brunch, but the similarity ends there. This one is truly romantic, excellently prepared, and reasonably priced at $14 per person.

Outdoor Kissing

KAANAPALI BEACH

Located off Highway 30, just north of Lahaina.

Without question, this magnificent stretch of soft sandy beach would unequivocally be the beach of choice on Maui if it weren't for the array of towering hotels and condominiums. Still, it is superior for swimming and walking through the surf at sunset.

Lahaina

Founded in the 1600s, Lahaina was once the capital of the Hawaiian Islands. Royalty was the focus of the town back then, with all the commensurate traditions and rituals. Later, from 1840 to 1860, Lahaina became an enterprising whaling port, with rowdy sailors and hundreds of ships coming and going yearly. It is hard to imagine those times as you walk along the crowded, tightly compact streets of this small village. Lahaina's monarchs and mariners are long gone, and the once-quaint community and energetic port has become a hodgepodge of T-shirt stores, jewelry boutiques, art galleries, clothing shops, oceanfront restaurants, and sightseeing boats. Visit anyway. There are several excellent restaurants here, and the view out to the water and harbor is exciting. Sip a maitai or piña colada in one of the many establishments along Front Street.

◆ **Romantic Note:** Many whale-watching charters depart from Lahaina between December and March, to witness the yearly migration of the humpback whales. It is almost impossible not to have a sighting, but even if you don't, you are likely to see dolphins, sea turtles, and other phenomenal sights.

Hotel/Bed and Breakfast Kissing

LAHAINA HOTEL, Lahaina
127 Lahainaluna Road
(808) 661-0577, (800) 669-3444
Inexpensive to Moderate

From Highway 30, turn west onto Lahainaluna Road.

Victorian elegance is rare in Hawaii, but it lavishly exists here at the Lahaina Hotel. A stunning, authentic renovation has turned this 13-room inn into a fascinating, sumptuous place to stay. Each room is affectionately decorated with floral wallpaper, lace draperies, stately antiques, eyelet bedspreads, crystal decanters filled with port wine, and attractive tile and marble bathrooms. Private balconies overlook the bustling town center, not exactly romantic, but a fact of life in this area. Some of the less expensive rooms are on the snug side, but still beautifully appointed. A simple continental breakfast is served on a buffet table in the common area. Trays are provided to take back to your room for a truly intimate repast.

◆ **Romantic Note:** The Romantic Note for the Plantation Inn (reviewed elsewhere in this section) applies here too, except the Lahaina Hotel does not have a swimming pool.

LAHAINA SHORES BEACH RESORT, Lahaina
475 Front Street
(800) 628-6699
Inexpensive to Unbelievably Expensive

From Highway 30 in the town of Lahaina, turn west onto Dickenson Street, drive until it dead-ends at Front Street, and turn right.

This stately plantation-style mansion turned resort rests on a wide sandy beach, far enough from the town center of Lahaina to make it a retreat that stands alone with the palm trees. That makes it sound more exotic than it is, but this lovely 200-room property is well worth your consideration. The rooms are capacious, with towering ceilings, simple but comfortable furnishings, full kitchens, and wide lanais; many feature outstanding ocean views. Studio and one-bedroom units are available. The pool is fine and the ocean swimming is even better. This isn't luxury, but it is out of the mainstream and meets all the requirements for a Hawaiian getaway.

PLANTATION INN, Lahaina
174 Lahainaluna Road
(808) 667-9225, (800) 433-6815
Inexpensive to Moderate

From Highway 30 turn west onto Lahainaluna Road.

How utterly refreshing to have such a place to stay on Maui. There are only 18 rooms in this country-elegant, sparkling clean, plantation-style bed and breakfast. All of the rooms have sensuous, plush furnishings and fabrics, hardwood floors, stained glass windows, bay and French windows, private verandas, canopy beds, VCRs, daily maid service, and central air-conditioning. Attention to service seems evident in the immaculate surroundings and the care the staff takes to see to your every need. Outside you'll find a large lovely pool, an immaculate garden area, and a whimsical open-air common room where cookies and coffee are served all day. A generous continental breakfast is served in the hotel's dining room, **GERARD'S** (reviewed elsewhere in this section).

◆　**Romantic Warning:** The inn is in the heart of Lahaina, which means the intensity of this hectic town center is outside your front door. There are no views to be had here and the nearest beach is a few miles up the road in Kaanapali. Having said that, let me reassure you that inside your room or at poolside there is little evidence any world exists at all except the luxurious one you are enjoying at the moment.

Restaurant Kissing

AVALON RESTAURANT, Lahaina　◆◆◀
844 Front Street
(808) 667-5559
Moderate to Expensive

From Highway 30 in the town of Lahaina, turn west onto Dickenson Street, drive until it dead-ends at Front Street, and turn right. The restaurant is at the back of a small courtyard of stores.

Set at the back of a small brick courtyard, somewhat away from the jam-packed main street of Lahaina, is this charming oasis of Indonesian and Asian cuisine. Actually, it isn't far enough away from the masses to be intimate, but the food and setting are delightful and the savory offerings worth the culinary diversion from true romance. The noodles in ginger sauce or garlic black bean sauce are delicious, whole fresh opakapaka is beautifully presented, and the Szechwan cream pasta with scallops and sun-dried tomatoes is distinctive.

DAVID PAUL'S LAHAINA GRILL, Lahaina　◆◆◆
127 Lahainaluna Road
(808) 667-5117
Moderate for lunch, Expensive for dinner

From Highway 30, turn west onto Lahainaluna Road.

Count on friendly, attentive service and superior, creative cooking at this sleek, bistro-style restaurant. The bold black-and-white-tiled floor, colorfully painted plates, and cozy tables draped in white linen fill the small dining room with drama. A varied menu includes a robust cioppino, a surprisingly authentic Caesar salad, and a light, fragrant vegetable paella they call *paellita*. Coffee lovers may want to try the roasted lamp chops marinated in Kona coffee and served with a hearty Kona coffee sauce.

GERARD'S, Lahaina   ❖❖❖
174 Lahainaluna Road, in the Plantation Inn
(808) 667-9225, (800) 433-6815
Expensive to Unbelievably Expensive

From Highway 30, turn west onto Lahainaluna Road.

Petite, quaint restaurants are hard to find in Hawaii: the large-scale hotels here like to emphasize affluence and grandeur. That is all fine and well, but it is a breath of fresh air to be able to relax in a gracious setting on an old-fashioned veranda, replete with wicker furnishings, to enjoy a cornucopia of savory French delights. You won't be disappointed with any of the selections. Our quails stuffed with truffles and foie gras, and the shiitake and oyster mushrooms in a light pastry shell were both perfect. Prices are steep—entrées start at $26 and top out at $48—so consider this one for only the most special of celebrations.

KIMO'S, Lahaina   ❖❖
831 Front Street
(808) 661-3472
Moderate

From Highway 30 in the town of Lahaina, turn west onto Dickenson Street, drive until it dead-ends at Front Street, and turn right.

It isn't the most romantic setting we've ever seen, but the service is amiable and the view above Front Street looking out to the water is spectacular. The open-air dining room has an affectionate, rustic quality, accented by beamed ceilings and high-backed colonial-style chairs. The casual menu features generous well-prepared portions of steak and extremely fresh seafood. Try any of their fresh fish coated with Parmesan cheese and breadcrumbs and topped with a lemon-caper butter—delicious.

◆ **Romantic Note: LAHAINA FISH CO.,** 831 Front Street, Lahaina, (808) 661-3472, (Moderate), isn't romantic and can actually get a bit rowdy, but the view directly out to the water makes it great for drinks sometime after lunch and before dinner, when the crowds are someplace else.

Kihei

What can happen to paradise when you pave it without consideration for the natural beauty of the area is vividly on display in Kihei. One high-rise condominium complex after another sprawls along a once-spectacular sweep of beach. The beach is actually still magnificent, but the landscape has been indelibly changed and the traffic through town can be a nightmare. Most of the properties in Kihei are standard condo units, some with views, many directly on the beach, all with pools, and most without air-conditioning. Some of the best bargains around are located in this part of the island, but for the most part you should look elsewhere for a romantic Hawaiian respite.

◆ **Romantic Note:** Kihei marks the border of the dry section of the island. In a typical year only 10 to 15 inches of water fall here. The arid conditions contribute to the barren landscape, but mean fewer days spent indoors during the rainy season.

Hotel/Bed and Breakfast Kissing

MANA KAI-MAUI, Kihei   💋
2960 South Kihei Road
(808) 879-1561, (800) 525-2025
Inexpensive (rates include rental car)

Call for directions.

At the southernmost end of Kihei, looking out to the idyllic beaches of Wailea and Makena, this high-rise condominium building is an inexpensive place to enjoy great views and a sweeping sandy beach. The furnishings are comfortable, and every unit has a small but usable lanai with extensive views of the water and Haleakala. Don't expect much; these basic but immaculate studio, one-, and two-bedroom condos are in need of renovation. Still, the views are stellar and the building is run more like a hotel, with its own activity center, gift shops, and the **OCEAN TERRACE RESTAURANT** (reviewed elsewhere in this section).

SUGAR BEACH RESORT, Kihei   ◆◀
2439 South Kihei Road
(808) 879-2778, (800) 367-5242
Inexpensive to Moderate

Call for directions.

This low-rise condominium complex, one of the more attractive buildings in Kihei, has a large number of nicely furnished, reasonably priced oceanfront units. Located directly on a grassy knoll just above an expansive, gentle beach area, Sugar Beach offers full kitchens, standard bathrooms, large lanais, and a great pool area. It's worth looking into.

◆   **Romantic Note:** Four or five different condominium rental companies represent the various owners of Sugar Beach. The prices are all pretty much the same and they all offer impressive vacation packages with car rental. A minimum stay is required.

Restaurant Kissing

OCEAN TERRACE RESTAURANT, Kihei   ◗
2960 South Kihei Road
(808) 879-2607
Inexpensive to Moderate

Call for directions.

This reasonably priced oceanfront restaurant rests just above water's edge, and the open-air dining room with terrace seating is actually quite attractive. The service could be described as island casual, but it is also somewhat indifferent. The standard menu offers basic, hearty breakfasts, salads and sandwiches for lunch, and steak and fish for dinner. The views remain steadfast: simply beautiful.

◆ **Romantic Warning:** The bar at the entrance to the restaurant has a rather loud television and is filled with smoke. Hold your breath as you walk by; the atmosphere inside is totally unrelated.

Wailea

In many ways Wailea is the premier destination on Maui. Unlike the developments at Kaanapali, which are squished together with very little breathing room, Wailea's series of prestige hotel and condominium developments are quite spread out. You couldn't say that it isn't crowded here, and the shore is indeed obscured by these super resorts, but it isn't anywhere near as dense as Kaanapali. Plus, the resorts are absolutely some of the sexiest places to stay on the island, and the beaches are simply awesome. The major hotels in this area line up along a mile of premier beachfront like five sisters posing for a picture: Kea Alani, Stouffer Beach Resort Wailea, Four Seasons Resort Wailea, Maui Inter-Continental Wailea, and the prettiest sibling, Grand Hyatt Wailea. It is hard to imagine being disappointed with any of them.

Those who have golf clubs or tennis racquets along can try to reserve time at the famous Wailea Golf Course, (808) 879-2966, or the 14-court Wailea Tennis Club, (808) 879-1958. But no matter where you stay, the entire area is one big playground for those who can afford to play.

◆ **Romantic Note:** The beaches along this area are some of the most beautiful on Hawaii. They are somewhat difficult to reach around the massive hotels, but they are accessible. Remember, all beaches in Hawaii are available for use by the public

Hotel/Bed and Breakfast Kissing

FOUR SEASONS, Wailea
3900 Wailea Alanui Drive
(808) 874-8000, (800) 334-6284
Unbelievably Expensive and Beyond

Just off Highway 31, in the town of Wailea.

After a while one grandiose place begins to look like another,
with all the same stellar amenities and superior services. However,
the Four Seasons stands out for its fine assortment of guest rooms
appointed with marble baths, soaking tubs, and separate glass
showers; a fabulously elegant pool area with private cabanas lining
the edge; and great restaurants, all bursting with romantic flair. Try
SEASONS restaurant, (808) 874-8000, (Very Expensive), for
superior dining in a luxurious setting. The **PACIFIC GRILL**,
(808) 874-8000, (Very Expensive), serves more casual meals, but
is also first-rate.

The oceanfront rooms are the best and the courtyard views are
the least interesting, but the property is set far away from water's
edge, making ocean watching from any room difficult. Still, the
surroundings are gilt-edged and worth your wholehearted consideration.

GRAND HYATT WAILEA, Wailea
3859 Wailea Alanui Drive
(808) 875-1234, (800) 888-6100
Unbelievably Expensive and Beyond

Just off Highway 31, in the town of Wailea.

There is little argument that the Grand Hyatt Wailea is the
ultimate resort spa in Hawaii and possibly the world. This may
seem to be an exaggeration, but in fact it may be an understatement. Six hundred million dollars' worth of sheer opulence and
grandeur dazzle you at every turn.

This phenomenal property has details that exceed your wildest
fantasies or earnest desires for pleasure seeking. From the immense

pool (and I mean immense), which features intricate mosaics with gold flecks and an elaborate series of slides and canals, to the world-class **SPA GRANDE**, with every possible therapy for the body you can imagine, to the multimillion-dollar art collection in the **BOTERO BAR**, to the fact that each floor has its own butler on call, this is Fantasy Island come true. (By the way, the butler is truly there for your every whim; one woman said her butler ironed her blouse and skirt, another couple had their butler draw their evening bath.) You can even order an extremely private multicourse dinner served by your own personal waiter on your lanai. Now that's romantic.

As you might expect, dining at this palace is a lavish experience. A near-legendary Japanese restaurant called **KINCHA** (Unbelieveably Expensive) has more than 800 tons of rock from Mount Fuji built into the foundation and surrounding gardens. The **GRAND DINING ROOM**, with its soaring ceilings, open-air dining, and 40-foot-high murals, is literally sublime. The thatched-roofed **HUMUHUMUNUKUNUKUAPUA'A** (don't ask me to pronounce it, it was hard enough to spell) floats on a massive saltwater lagoon where tropical fish thrive. And there's more, but you should see this all for yourselves.

Did I forget to mention the rooms? Sumptuously appointed in upscale hotel style, they are still basically hotel rooms—but not as outstanding as everything else around you. Ocean views look out over the pool, and they are the most coveted and expensive in the resort. Actually, the most expensive suite in the world is located at this Grand Hyatt. For $8,500 a night you too can live in the lap of luxury, but only if some sultan or celebrity hasn't beaten you to the punch. But that seems like a minor grievance in the midst of all this awesome refinement and service. Every staff member seems genuinely concerned about your stay.

There's also an utterly quaint wedding chapel, set in the middle of a tropical garden and a freshwater pond. The stained glass windows depicting handsome Polynesians in repose radiate golden light with the movement of the sun. As many as 60 weddings a month take place here. If you're considering making your vows

here, the Hyatt's wedding director can help create the wedding of
your dreams, maybe even beyond your dreams.

◆   **Romantic Note:** Children in tow rarely make for a romantic escape, but if you happen to have the little darlings along, the
Hyatt offers a 20,000-square-foot wonderland of day care. A
computer room, theater, soda shop, arts-and-crafts room with
pottery wheels, video-game room, infant care center, and a wonderful outdoor playground provide supervised fun for the younger
set. For $35 a day (evenings are extra) you may want to come here
and play awhile yourselves.

KEA ALANI, Wailea
4100 Wailea Alanui Drive
(808) 875-4100, (800) 659-4100
Unbelievably Expensive and Beyond
Just off Highway 31, in the town of Wailea.

Describing the exterior of this massive hotel might distract you
from the real story inside its 22 acres of tropical elegance, but you
should know about it before you arrive. The glaringly white
building has a pattern of immense Dairy Queen swirls sitting on top
of the roof. They're supposed to look something like a mosque,
although some people think they resemble huge white breasts.
Whatever they are, they are conspicuously strange, but once you're
inside they are also soon forgotten.

The rooms at the Kea Alani are stunning and plush. In all price
categories, every room is an impressive suite with curved doorways,
separate bedroom, two televisions, stereo, VCR and laser disc
player, large tiled bath with soaking tub, two sinks, marble appointments, and wide lanai complete with a lounge chair and table. In
some ways this is just another of the massive hotel properties lining
the beaches of Wailea, but that is saying a lot. A splendid multilevel pool area with a 140-foot slide and dotted with private
cabanas, a wonderfully silky sandy beach, excellent outdoor dining, magnificent common areas for quiet conversation, and supe-

rior service are all here. But the Kea Alani's base price starts at almost $100 less than its expensive neighbors. It's still expensive, but it is utterly wonderful.

Breakfast, lunch, and dinner are served in the exquisite open-air dining room called **KEA ALANI—THE RESTAURANT** (Moderate to Expensive). Fashioned in a grand hall style with towering arched windows and ceiling, it is a stunning place to dine. The menu lists an interesting mix of Mediterranean and continental cuisine. Most of it is quite good and the fresh fish is always moist and tender.

CIAO (Inexpensive) is a delightful casual eatery with elegant Corinthian columns, marble flooring, and only a handful of wrought-iron tables. Excellent cappuccinos and the best pastries on Maui are here for a light breakfast, lunch, or snack almost any time of day. What a shame it is located in such a hard-to-find section of the Kea Alani.

MAUI INTER-CONTINENTAL WAILEA, Wailea   ◆◀
3700 Wailea Alanui Drive
(808) 879-1922, (800) 367-2960
Moderate to Unbelievably Expensive and Beyond

Just off Highway 31, in the town of Wailea.

The Inter-Continental is in need of substantial renovations, but there are a few good reasons to make this your romantic destination in Hawaii. The prices in the nonview rooms are among the most reasonable for any major beachfront resort in Hawaii, and all of the amenities are here: an OK pool area, sandy beach, rather good restaurants, and attentive service. The rooms are decent—the ones with views out to the water are the best—but they all show their age and lack of care. In the meantime, until the owners find the money to bring it up to par with its preeminent neighbors, it is one of the better bargains on the beach.

STOUFFER WAILEA BEACH RESORT, Wailea
3550 Wailea Alanui Drive
(808) 879-4900, (800) 992-4532
Expensive to Unbelievably Expensive and Beyond

Just off Highway 31, in the town of Wailea.

A multimillion-dollar renovation has turned this Stouffer into a showcase of refinement and superior accommodations. The sizable rooms are attractively decorated in soft neutral tones of beige and taupe, and appointed with wicker love seats, cane coffee tables, large lanais with cushioned wrought-iron chairs and tables, and attractive tile baths. Winding pathways dotted with intriguing statues and lush gardens take you down to the pool and pristine Mokapu Beach. Because of the way the property is situated, the ocean-view rooms have poor visibility out to the magical waters of the Pacific. This is one of the few places where a water-oriented room may not be the prize of the resort. Most of the other rooms have rather rich tropical vistas.

It is tough to decide between the Stouffer's distinguished restaurants, **RAFFLES** and the **PALM COURT** (both are reviewed elsewhere in this section); each is excellent and the venues are superb. So forget deciding—dine at the Palm Court for lunch and Raffles for dinner. Your taste buds and hearts will be eternally grateful.

THE VILLAS AT WAILEA, Wailea
Reservation office: 3750 Wailea Alanui Drive
(808) 879-1595, (800) 367-5246
Moderate to Unbelievably Expensive

Call for directions.

These four sprawling, private townhouse villages are scattered around the beachfront area of Wailea. They aren't grand, but the attractive units provide an affordable alternative to the excesses of Wailea's huge hotels. One other drawback: the feeling is somewhat cramped, with front doors or lanais facing one another, and the pool areas are small. Still, the homey surroundings do create a relaxing place to stay.

Miscellaneous Kissing

SPA GRANDE, Wailea ◆◆◆◆
3859 Wailea Alanui Drive, in the Grand Hyatt Wailea
(808) 875-1234, (800) 888-6100
Moderate to Unbelievably Expensive

Just off Highway 31, in the town of Wailea.

Imagine having two massage therapists working on your weary, appreciative body at the same time. Or being massaged side-by-side with your beloved, followed by a relaxing private herbal bath *à deux*. Body facials, all forms of hydra therapy, and total beauty treatments are performed in an amazing marble-ensconced forum. Here you can try the extraordinary "Terme Wailea" (women and men have their own separate areas for this one). You start with a Japanese-style bath or loofah scrub, proceeded by a plunge into a hot mineral tub, then a cool one, followed by steam, sauna, a waterfall shower, a unique herbal bath, and then a seemingly jet-powered shower. Fees start at $75 a day for nonguests and $40 for guests. Combinations can total into the hundreds of dollars, depending on what indulgences you choose. You won't have the energy to kiss after this experience, but holding each other close for hours afterwards will be sheer bliss.

Upcountry

On the northeastern slopes of Haleakala, a different facet of island life is on display for those who can bear to leave the beach. Upcountry Kula is where you'll find the last remnants of true "local" life on the islands. Other small country hamlets such as Makawao are slowly (and reluctantly) making the transition from 1968 to 1993. An eclectic assortment of restaurants and country shops line Western-style streets. Some are strictly bohemian, while others are urbane enough to sell lattes and designer ceramics.

As you drive farther on, away from the crowds, you climb up undulating hills covered with emerald green fields and dotted with patches of chaparral. Horses, cattle, and farm crops thrive here. At the end of the road is **TEDESCHI VINEYARDS**, (808) 878-6058, the only commercial winery in Hawaii. Tours and wine tastings are available (the pineapple wine is better than it sounds) and the setting exquisite.

Upcountry weather is entirely different from the coast's. In the winter, evening temperatures can drop into the 40s and rain can be persistent. But the views are spellbinding and the country calm is superlative. No high-rise or condominium developments exist for miles around. This may just be paradise.

Makawao

Hotel/Bed and Breakfast Kissing

McKAY COTTAGE, Makawao   ◆◆◆
Reservations through Hawaii's Best Bed and Breakfast
(800) 885-0550
Inexpensive

Call for directions.

Of all the bed and breakfasts on Maui (there aren't many), this is by far the most private and affectionate. Eucalyptus trees and a vast array of protea blossoms embrace this engaging cottage. Floral fabrics, balloon valances, wicker furnishings, a separate bedroom, brick fireplace (evenings at the 4,000-foot level of Mount Haleakala can necessitate curling up before a glowing fire), and a well-stocked kitchen, complete with morning treats, are all delightful and homey, although not all homes are this cozy. A French door leads out to the stunning scenery and a compelling view of the ocean. The owners can even arrange an exclusive hike and/or picnic on the ranch lands.

Restaurant Kissing

CASANOVA, Makawao
1188 Makawao Avenue
(808) 572-0220
Inexpensive

Call for directions.

It's not easy to accommodate many tastes and styles without appearing confused and awkward, but somehow this attractive Italian eatery pulls it off. The front half of the restaurant is a somewhat smoke-filled bar where locals hang out while waiting for the music to begin. Anything from traditional folk music to reggae may be the special entertainment for the evening; sets start at 9:00 p.m. and continue into the wee hours. The back half of the restaurant holds a series of tables snugly grouped together where you can indulge in appetizing Italian cuisine. Fresh bread, hearty portions, and efficient service are all standard at Casanova. Although the real Casanova had the reputation of being fickle, this namesake is always reliable.

◆ **Romantic Alternative: COURTYARD DELI**, 3620 Baldwin Avenue, Makawao, (808) 572-3456, (Inexpensive), is a tiny eatery just down the street from Casanova. Great lattes, fresh baked pastries, and a small selection of sandwiches are all delicious.

Haiku

Hotel/Bed and Breakfast

PILIALOHA, Haiku
255 Kaupakalua Road
(808) 572-1440
Inexpensive

Call for directions.

A lone cottage adjacent to the owners' home crowns an acre of green lawn surrounded by a thick evergreen and eucalyptus forest. Everything is immaculate and affectionately decorated, with modest yet comfortable furnishings and a beautifully stocked kitchen filled with breakfast goodies. Beach chairs, picnic coolers, floats, snorkel equipment, and blankets are available to make any outing hassle-free. It may not be the beach, but this is every inch a romantic getaway.

Kula

Hotel/Bed and Breakfast Kissing

AHINAAHINA FARM BED AND BREAKFAST, ◆◆◀
Kula
210 Ahinaahina Place
(808) 878-6096
Inexpensive

Call for directions.

Set amidst bountiful citrus, banana, and fruit trees on the slopes of Kula, overlooking the crystal blue Pacific in the distance, is this appealing two-cottage bed and breakfast. Well spaced from each other as well as the owners' home, both units have charming natural wood construction and are exceedingly picturesque, with bright simple interiors, comfortable furnishings and large covered decks that take full advantage of the view down to the coast and water in the distance. The full kitchen is packed with a generous continental breakfast, and a washer and dryer are available. Warm vests and windbreakers are provided if you want to hike Mount Haleakala.

Hana

The road to heavenly Hana has saved this remote section of Maui from becoming overdeveloped, or indeed developed at all.

More than any other area of the major islands, this is the way Hawaii used to be. The best way to describe the excursion to Hana by car is "death by driving." There are at least 52 hairpin turns in what most people would call an unpassable road. Another hazard is the unpredictable road repairs, which cause unbelievable backups and delays. Despite these conditions, almost 2,000 people arrive in hundreds of cars daily, including sight-seeing vans by the dozens.

What could be so enthralling to cause such a caravan? The main highlight is the **SEVEN POOLS** (Oheo Gulch), a freshwater swimming hole with a cascading waterfall and the endless Pacific beyond. This is the kind of scenery most of us see only in the movies. Also, the drive itself is a wondrous journey through a rain forest, replete with remarkable panoramas.

Is Hana worth the trip? This pristine town of only a few hundred people in tropical surroundings with staggering views of the countryside and Pacific makes an enchanting backdrop for a heart-stirring getaway. If you come early enough (allow two hours for the drive from most points on the island) or late enough in the day and stay at least a night or two, it is more than worth the drive, and there are many other spots to discover besides the Seven Pools. **HAMOA BEACH** is a lovely gray sand beach in the town center; **WAILUA FALLS**, seven miles outside of town, is a cascading waterfall ending in a clear blue pool. **WAI'ANAPANAPA STATE PARK** has a black sand beach and camping. An ancient footpath winds along the rugged coastline, where you can witness blow holes and sea caves. From all perspectives, Hana is probably the most romantic town on Maui.

◆ **Romantic Note:** Hana doesn't offer much in the way of dining or shopping; the outdoors is the attraction here and little else. The only restaurants and main accommodations in town are at the **HOTEL HANA-MAUI** (reviewed elsewhere in this section). Other lodgings include home and condominium rentals. Bring a picnic with you, as well as towels and your swimwear, and take a plunge in the waters, both fresh and salt, when the mood seems right.

◆ **Romantic Suggestion:** On your way to and from Hana, you might want to consider stopping at **MAMA'S FISH HOUSE,** 799 Poho, Kuau, (808) 579-8488, (Moderate to Expensive), for lunch or dinner. The casual wood interior is filled with exuberance, and the kitchen has consistently served great fresh fish dishes for 30 years. The view of the water and nearby rocky beach is dazzling.

Hotel/Bed and Breakfast Kissing

HALE MALAMALAMA, Hana
Reservations through Hawaii's Best Bed and Breakfast
(800) 262-9912
Moderate to Expensive (breakfast not included)

Call for directions.

Spend affectionate time together in Hana while staying in a duplex cottage divided into the Garden Suite downstairs and the Royal Suite upstairs, or in the nearby Treehouse Cottage. Surrounded by lush tropical foliage, each unit has wood detailing, comfortable furnishings, private decks, and a complete kitchen. The Treehouse Cottage has views of the water, and a large Jacuzzi tub designed for two that is perfect for couples looking for unrivaled privacy.

HANA-ALI'I HOLIDAYS, Hana
(800) 548-0478, (808) 248-7742
Moderate to Very Expensive

Call for directions to the individual rentals.

A small number of cottages and homes in a range of sizes and conditions are available for rental through Hana-Ali'i Holidays. Set up housekeeping in one and soak up the tropical bliss.

We recommend several from their eclectic selection. **EKENA** is a stunning, spacious hillside estate with panoramic views of the coast and countryside. Comfortable furnishings, a television and VCR, plus a washer and dryer make this an enviable place to stay. **PARADISE HIDEAWAY** rests on a five-acre flower farm complete with hot tub, swimming pool, sparkling ocean views, and enough space for you and two other romantic couples. It is truly one of the most beautiful homes in Hana. **HONOKALANI COT-TAGE** is a charming wood-frame bungalow with a wraparound deck that takes full advantage of the ocean view and the lush tropical setting. The open one-room layout is delightful. **HALE HANA BAY** is a petite oceanfront cottage that has imposing views from the deck and living room. Comfort abounds and all the amenities are here, including privacy and lush surroundings.

◆   **Romantic Note:** Minimum stays can vary from three days to a week.

HANA PLANTATION HOUSES, Hana
(800) 657-7723, (808) 248-7248
Moderate to Very Expensive

Call for directions to the individual rentals.

This agency is known for its exceptionally discriminating selection of cottages and homes to rent in the Hana area. It is an understatement to say that each one is distinctive and unique; most are fabulous, and it is hard to go wrong. Many of the homes are large with grand views and tropical settings. Fully equipped kitchens, TV/VCR, outdoor Jacuzzis, cozy living rooms, full baths, and private lanais are some of the amenities available. They even offer a solar-powered cottage near Hana Bay. Premier among the properties is the **PLANTATION HOUSE**, poised on an acre of tropical gardens, surrounded by outstanding views from two cov-ered lanais, and rich in all the posh, comfy details required for an exclusive respite.

◆   **Romantic Note:** Minimum stays can vary from three days to a week.

HOTEL HANA-MAUI, Hana
(808) 248-8211, (800) 321-HANA
Unbelievably Expensive and Beyond

Take the road to Hana and follow the signs to the hotel.

For all intents and purposes this is literally the only game in town when it comes to anything in the way of hotel accommodations and restaurants, and it has been like that forever. Inaccessibility is the main, if not only, reason for the lack of competition, because everything else about this area is spectacular.

Hotel Hana-Maui has an august 40-year history, and was once owned by millionairess Carolyn Hunt. Her taste and style are still apparent in the sumptuous bungalows and cottages scattered over the Hana hillside. Oversized plush furnishings, comfy beds, roomy baths with walk-in tile showers and soaking tubs, and floor-to-ceiling sliding glass doors that open to your own private patio are all polished and sophisticated. Many of the 96 units also have handsome lawn furniture, views, and hot tubs. The wonderful large pool area overlooks rolling lawns and the ocean in the distance. The beaches aren't easily accessible, but the hotel provides a shuttle to a stretch of gray sand about a mile away. The isolation and the luxury are what make this place so captivating. You'd be hard put to find anything quite like the Hotel Hana-Maui anywhere else in Hawaii.

◆ **Romantic Warning:** After all these words of praise, we have a few critical warnings you must know about before you get too excited about the Hotel Hana-Maui. Despite the restaurants' intriguing setting, the kitchen here serves some of the poorest food we've ever sampled. The hamburger made McDonald's seem like haute cuisine, and the undercooked pasta had a tomato sauce that tasted like ketchup. After that we didn't even bother risking dinner. It's almost embarrassing, and at these prices it's actually near criminal. Also, since the Sheraton started managing the hotel two years ago, the formerly attentive service has gone downhill. You could wait a long time at poolside before someone gets you a towel or offers a drink.

◆ **Romantic Note:** A short, tricky walk away from the hotel is a small, secluded red sand beach. Lava rocks at the opening of this bay keep the waters calm, while the surging ocean crashes against the large boulders. Early in the morning you are likely to be the only ones here, but later in the day some of the locals and other guests often find their way down.

Kauai

> "...kisses are a better fate than wisdom."
>
> e.e. cummings

KAUAI

It's no wonder Kauai is called the "Garden Isle." Kauai's landscape is sheer poetry, burgeoning with fruit trees of every kind, brilliant-colored tropical flowers, fertile valleys, breathtaking mountains and canyons, and pristine sandy beaches. Bougainvillea blossoms in colorful abundance along the roadside, palm fronds sway high in the coconut trees, and acres upon acres of sugarcane rustle in the trade winds.

On September 11, 1992, this tranquil island paradise was transformed by the most devastating natural disaster in Hawaii's recorded history: Hurricane Iniki, the second hurricane to strike Kauai in the past ten years. Hurricane Iwa, which struck Kauai in 1982, was mild in comparison to Iniki. Iniki's fury, although short-lived, will never be forgotten, and few were spared from her reign of destruction. The island was literally defoliated in the storm and nearly 50 percent of the island's homes were damaged, if not altogether destroyed. Especially in the coastal areas, winds lifted roofs off houses, while beaches, roads, homes, hotels, and more were tossed, crushed, and destroyed by raging winds and waves.

Fortunately, Mother Nature and the human spirit are resilient, and within months the flora and fauna, as well as tourists, began to return. Only seven months after the hurricane, Kauai's lush landscape revealed few traces of the hurricane's ruin. However, buildings and streets are not so easily replaced. Damaged roads, parks, beaches, resorts, and homes await repairs, particularly along the coastline. Beachfront properties are still strewn with rubble and debris; some are posted with "for sale" signs. Interestingly, the storm displaced many beaches, so while beaches in some areas have been lost, new beaches have been gained elsewhere.

Over time, extensive community effort has rebuilt homes and replaced roofs. Numerous hotels have been repaired and are back in operation, and many who were evacuated are home again, but the progress and healing are slow going. Many more hotels are still under construction and not even close to reopening. Further delaying the restoration process, insurance companies, inundated with claims, have been unable to pay for the present disaster, not to mention unwilling (and unable) to reissue disaster insurance.

So, the question remains for those looking for a tropical romantic interlude, should you travel to Kauai? Categorically the answer is yes! Kauai is still one of the most stunning places on earth, and, miraculously, Hurricane Iniki has done little to change this. Your lodging and dining options are somewhat limited until restorations are complete, but the places that have reopened are better than ever. For updates on what is and isn't open, call the **KAUAI HOTLINE** at (800) 262-1400.

West Shore

The west shore consists of several nondescript residential towns dotting the coast and offers little in terms of dining and lodging for tourists. Nevertheless, you'll want to make a day trip here (if not several) to view some of the west shore's natural wonders, including the breathtaking Waimea Canyon and beautiful sandy beaches.

Waimea

Hotel/Bed and Breakfast Kissing

WAIMEA PLANTATION COTTAGES, Waimea   ◗◖
9600 Kaumualii Highway #367
(808) 338-1625, (800) 992-4632
Moderate to Expensive

From the Lihue Airport, follow Highway 50 west to Waimea. The cottages are on the left.

Sandwiched between the beach and highway, this former sugar plantation almost resembles a trailer park, but instead of trailers you'll find snug rows of cottages set on stilts lining an oceanfront lot. These picturesque former plantation workers' homes, dating back to the 1900s, are harbored on an intriguing black sand beach. All have been affectionately restored, with shady ocean-view verandas and cozy wicker porch furniture. The one-bedroom cottages have full kitchens, hardwood floors, and simple furnishings. The ones nearest the ocean are preferable: the beach is just yards from your lanai and there are no neighbors obstructing your view. Tennis courts and a small swimming pool are also available to guests.

◆ **Romantic Warning:** Far too many cottages are clustered on the property, but this is really the only romantic overnight option in Waimea. If you're interested in spending several days exploring the hiking trails and beaches in the area (and you should be—they're really worthwhile!), this is an affordable and comfortable place to rest weary feet and hearts.

◆ **Romantic Alternative:** KOKEE LODGE, Waimea Canyon Drive, Waimea, (808) 335-6061, (Very Inexpensive), offers rental cabins at the top of Waimea Canyon Drive. This is the only other lodging option in Waimea, but think twice about staying here. Service is gruff and wild roosters roam (and crow) freely. The only reason to rent one of these musky, run-down cabins is if you want do a lot of hiking and would prefer not to drive up and down the hill each day.

Restaurant Kissing

GROVE DINING ROOM, Waimea   ◀
9600 Kaumualii Highway, #367
(808) 338-1625
Inexpensive

From the Lihue Airport, follow Highway 50 west to Waimea. The dining room is at the Waimea Plantation Cottages, on the left.

This small dining room, set just off the highway behind the Waimea Plantation Cottages, serves very standard breakfasts, lunches, and dinners in an exceedingly unadorned dining room. The veranda, which provides views of the cottages and ocean in the distance, is the closest you can get to romantic dining in Waimea (and even this is stretching it!).

Outdoor Kissing

WAIMEA CANYON/KOKEE STATE PARK ◆◆◆◆
(808) 335-5871

Heading westbound on Highway 50, turn right onto Waimea Canyon Drive (Highway 550), or travel another three miles to Kekaha and turn uphill on Kokee Road, which later joins Waimea Canyon Drive. Either way, it is about a 40-minute drive.

"Grand Canyon of the Pacific," as Waimea Canyon has been dubbed, lives up to its nickname. A long twisting road journeys up 4,000 feet to stunning vistas that will surprise anyone who expected all of the Garden Isle's beauty to be found in its gardens. Make your first stop at the **WAIMEA CANYON LOOKOUT** to breathe in the fresh, cool air and admire the steep, verdant valleys contrasting with bare volcanic rock and rich red soil. A spectacular kaleidoscope of colors ranges from lush forest green to glowing crimson, depending on the weather and time of day. Continue up the hill and be sure to pause at the **PUU KA PELE** and **PUU HINAHINA** lookouts. Each stop offers another perspective on the canyon and is as magnificent as the last.

Proceed next to Kokee State Park, where you'll see a small museum and lodge, but stop here only if you're ravenous or need a hiking trail map; otherwise you'll be disappointed by the shabby facilities. Beyond there, both the **KALALAU** and the **PUU O KILA** lookouts are perched above a vast green landscape facing the shimmering blue ocean. The scene is so breathtaking, you may need mouth-to-mouth resuscitation. Hopefully you're with someone who can help.

◆   **Romantic Note:** Bring along comfortable shoes and a light jacket; the temperature at this altitude is quite cool but still pleasant and perfect for hiking. The many trails range from easy walks to rugged hikes, all with incredible scenery. For more information and trail maps, write to the **STATE DEPARTMENT OF LAND AND NATURAL RESOURCES**, 3060 Eiwa Street, #306, Lihue, Kauai, Hawaii 96766.

Mana

Outdoor Kissing

POLIHALE PARK BEACH, Mana

From Lihue Airport, follow Highway 50 south and then west, past the towns of Kekaha and Mana, until the highway ends. Turn onto the dirt road and follow signs to Polihale Park Beach.

Our curiosity was instantly piqued when we surveyed our map of Kauai and discovered that the highway along the west shore eventually turns into a dirt road, then ends altogether at Polihale Park Beach. Before we knew it, we found ourselves in search of this isolated beach. Despite the fact that the dirt road is well marked on the map, we wound our way several miles along the bumpy, potholed road with nothing but dry brush in sight and couldn't help but wonder if we had taken the wrong turnoff. To our sheer delight, after 15 minutes of dusty trying-to-be-patient driving, we finally came upon a velvety sand beach, set beneath the sheer cliffs of the Na Pali coastline. The sun had just sunk below the horizon, weaving a tapestry of colors across the sky, and we were held captive in the beauty of the moment and in each other's arms.

Polihale Beach is celebrated as one of Kauai's most beautiful beaches, which (to our disappointment) means it isn't really as much of a secret as the road might lead you to believe. Even so, the lengthy dirt road deters crowds, and the odds of having the beach to yourselves are in your favor.

South Shore

Kauai's south shore was once famous for extraordinary sand beaches and luxury hotels, but Hurricane Iniki was far from gentle with this splendid coastline. It will be several years before the south shore can emerge from its awesome state of disrepair, although beach restoration efforts are in progress.

Unfortunately, due to construction, we were unable to look at most of the hotels on this side of the island. Many are scheduled to reopen by 1994, although some are attempting to open earlier. In time, the south shore will reclaim its illustrious beauty, but until then lodging, dining, and sunbathing options are strictly limited.

Poipu

Hotel/Bed and Breakfast Kissing

COLONY'S POIPU KAI, Poipu
1941 Poipu Road
(808) 742-6464
Expensive

From the Lihue Airport, travel southwest on Highway 50 and turn left at the junction of Highways 50 and 520. Follow Highway 520 south to Poipu, where it turns into Poipu Road; the hotel is on the right.

The romantic possibilities are endless at Colony's Poipu Kai. In fact, there are so many options, it's difficult to decide which condominium to rent and which activities to enjoy. The five condominium subdivisions are scattered across 70 acres of well-manicured tropical grounds, close to the ocean. Be sure to request the spacious suites with ocean views, luxurious decor, and renovated interiors when making your reservations. The condominiums are *not* air-conditioned and are individually owned and decorated, which means the amenities, views, and decor can vary significantly from one to the next.

Six freshwater swimming pools, nine tennis courts, several barbecues, one Jacuzzi (it's hard to believe there's only one), and nearby golf courses are available for guests. At one time the property had access to Brenneke Beach, but the hurricane destroyed this once-famous stretch of shoreline. Until further repairs are made, swimming, surfing, and sunbathing here are out of the question.

◆ **Romantic Note:** These five condominium subdivisions are managed and rented by several different companies, but Colony's Poipu Kai is one of the few that offers daily maid service.

GRANTHAM RESORTS,
POIPU BEACH CONDOMINIUMS, Poipu
2721 Poipu Road
(808) 742-7220, (800) 325-5701
Moderate to Very Expensive

From the Lihue Airport, travel southwest on Highway 50 and turn left at the junction of Highways 50 and 520. Follow Highway 520 south to Poipu, where it turns into Poipu Road; the hotel is on the right.

Grantham Resorts is yet another vacation rental company offering a varied selection of luxury condominiums and private rental homes. The **WAIKOMO STREAM, NIHI KAI,** and **MAKAHUENA CONDOMINIUMS**, among other condominium complexes owned by Grantham Resorts, are spacious and pleasant, providing one-, two-, and three-bedroom suites, full kitchens, view lanais, swimming pools, tennis courts, and nearby golf courses; almost everything but air-conditioning. The more specific you are about requesting suites with ocean views and attractive decor, the happier you will be once you get there.

If you're in the mood for ultimate luxury and seclusion, consider one of Grantham's vacation homes. Prices range from Moderate to Very Expensive, depending on the style, amenities, and location. Many of these homes are simply spectacular and couldn't be more ideal for romantic encounters.

HYATT REGENCY, Poipu
1571 Poipu Road
(808) 742-1234, (800) 233-1234
Expensive to Unbelievably Expensive

From the Lihue Airport, travel southwest on Highway 50 and turn left at the junction of Highways 50 and 520. Follow Highway 520 south to Poipu, where it turns into Poipu Road; the hotel is on the right.

The Hyatt is the first major resort in this area to open since the hurricane, so it has few competitors (at least for now). Yet even when the other nearby hotels open, this is still likely to be your first choice—if your budget allows. Enveloped by 50 acres of jungle-like landscape, this palatial resort is designed to be reminiscent of Hawaii in the 1920s, with green tiled roofs and white stucco walls. Fronting the ocean and a sandy beach, the Hyatt claims to get the most sunshine of all the hotels in Kauai. Guests who want to take full advantage of the weather can do so in style: the Hyatt offers a five-acre saltwater lagoon, three pools (one winds through the tropical garden landscape while another has slides, waterfalls, and Jacuzzis), a nearby golf course, tennis courts, and riding stables. Plus ocean-view restaurants where you can hold hands and watch the waves. Yes, it really is as extravagant as it sounds!

Six hundred air-conditioned guest suites provide luxurious intimacy with tasteful plantation-style furnishings and attractive floral linens. Rooms without ocean views are less expensive and face the majestic Haupu mountain range. Oceanfront suites are preferable, but make sure yours isn't over the noisy Seaview Lounge. Clanking dishes and rowdy shouts are sure to detract from the otherwise perfectly romantic mood.

Restaurant Kissing

DONDERO'S, Poipu
1571 Poipu Road, in the Hyatt Regency
(808) 742-1234
Expensive

From the Lihue Airport, travel southwest on Highway 50 and turn left at the junction of Highways 50 and 520. Follow Highway 520 south to Poipu, where it turns into Poipu Road; the restaurant is on the right, in the Hyatt.

It's no surprise that Dondero's is full of intricate inlaid marble flooring, lovely green tilework, and beautiful surrounding murals of the Mediterranean countryside. This level of opulence is typical of the Hyatt. Although prices are steep, the service is impeccable, and you'll savor Kauai's finest Italian cuisine, from braised veal shank to grilled shrimp wrapped in pancetta.

◆ **Romantic Note: TIDEPOOLS** is the Hyatt's more casual dining alternative for those who want superior views of the sun setting over the ocean but don't want to spend a fortune. Guests dine in romantic grass-thatched Polynesian huts set near a peaceful lagoon. The unique surroundings (and relatively moderate prices) make dishes such as charred ahi, fresh lobster, and mud pie seem that much more delicious.

THE HOUSE OF SEAFOOD, Poipu
1941 Poipu Road
(808) 742-6433
Expensive

On Poipu Road, between Hoowili and Pee roads.

As the waiter rattled off the ten different types of fish, prepared ten different ways, confusion drove us to try the most exotic sounding entrées—not a wise choice. Creativity can be good, but the delicate flavor of the fish was lost in the confusion of too many ingredients. Service is casual, and the softly lit room, with tables set beside open windows, is lovely. They have good selection and variety, but the moral of the story is: stick to more basic dishes and always save room for dessert.

◆ **Romantic Alternative: PANCHO AND LEFTY'S**, 5330A Koloa Road, Koloa, (808) 742-7377, (Inexpensive), is a much more casual, but cheerful and colorful, alternative for both lunch and dinner. (Good lunch spots are especially hard to find on the south shore.) We recommend Pancho and Lefty's for the fresh Mexican food rather than tug-at-your-heartstrings ambience. The steak or chicken fajitas for two are tasty and about as romantic as it gets here.

ILIMA TERRACE, Poipu
1571 Poipu Road, in the Hyatt Regency
(808) 742-1234
Moderate

From the Lihue Airport, travel southwest on Highway 50 and turn left at the junction of Highways 50 and 520. Follow Highway 520 south to Poipu, where it turns into Poipu Road; the restaurant is on the right, in the Hyatt.

Treat yourselves to creative cuisine and spectacular ocean views in this breezy, open-air restaurant. High ceilings, weathered brass chandeliers, floral tablecloths, and wicker chairs set the mood for fresh, casual dining. The breakfast buffet is a cornucopia of tropical delights and the lunch menu offers unusual island treats including papaya and smoked tuna salad or salmon broiled and simmered in sake and soy sauce. Top off your meal with a cup of steaming Kona coffee, then wander through the Hyatt's lovely garden landscape for a kiss on the beach.

Outdoor Kissing

SHIPWRECK POINT, Poipu

From the Lihue Airport, travel southwest on Highway 50 and turn left at the junction of Highways 50 and 520. Follow Highway 520 south to Poipu, where it turns into Poipu Road; Shipwreck Point is on the right, near the Hyatt.

At the edge of the Hyatt's property you'll find a dramatic lookout where the ocean meets a rocky cliff. Cliff diving is said to be popular here, but we didn't see any brave souls trying it. We preferred to play it safe and witness the glorious sunset instead.

East Shore

Believe it or not, even Kauai has traffic, and you're most likely to get caught in it on the east shore. The highway here runs along the overdeveloped coast, which is crowded with hotels, gas stations, restaurants, houses, and even more hotels. The advantage of this area is its extremely affordable hotels and restaurants, but unfortunately many of these aren't something we would recommend for intimate encounters. But don't give up on the east shore altogether. We discovered some wonderful places to kiss, despite the traffic.

Hanamaulu

Restaurant Kissing

HANAMAULU CAFÉ, Hanamaulu
Kuhio Highway (Highway 56)
(808) 245-3225
Moderate

From the Lihue Airport, head north on Highway 570, then follow Highway 56 north to Hanamaulu. The restaurant is on the right.

Upon entering, you may wonder if we are serious about recommending this place. Venture beyond the tacky front dining area though, and you'll be pleasantly surprised by the five shoji-screened tea rooms that are situated around a lush Japanese garden and koi pond. Slip off your shoes, pull up a cushion, and sit Japanese-style (or stretch out your legs, there's plenty of room under the table) and enjoy this lovely scene while you wait to be served. Unfortunately, the wait can be long because service is slow.

Order a nine-course Chinese or Japanese meal to sample a plentiful variety of dishes such as crispy-fried ginger chicken, sweet-and-sour spare-ribs, and chop suey with noodles. The courses are fresh and not greasy, but also just average. Reservations are requested—make sure you ask to be seated in the back.

◆ **Romantic Warning:** If you aren't lucky enough to be the only couple seated in one of the tea rooms, seating is far too close for comfort. An earlier dinner might offer a bit more privacy, but by the time you read your fortune cookie things are likely to be downright hectic.

Kapaa

Hotel/Bed and Breakfast Kissing

WAILUA BAY VIEW CONDOMINIUMS, Kapaa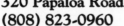
320 Papaloa Road
(808) 823-0960
Moderate

Follow the Kuhio Highway (Highway 56) north into Kapaa. The condominium complex is on the right.

Once you've experienced the affordable privacy and comfort to be had here, you'll wonder why the nearby hotels get any business at all. If it weren't for the busy highway and ceaseless roar of the cars that run behind this condominium complex, the Wailua Bay View would be an even better find. These individually owned and decorated one-bedroom apartments front the beach and offer exquisite ocean views. In winter and early spring you're likely to sight whales in the distance or sea turtles swimming along the shore. Each unit has been beautifully restored, providing a spacious full kitchen, splendid ocean view, and tasteful, luxurious decor that has been embellished with the owners' personal touches.

◆ **Romantic Alternative:** Interestingly, the **KAPAA SHORE OCEANFRONT RESORT CONDOMINIUMS**, 4-900 Kuhio Highway, Kapaa, (808) 822-3055, (Moderate), are nearly identical in structure to the Wailua Bay View rentals just up the street. These, too, are sandwiched between the highway and ocean and provide affordable ocean-view accommodations. Individually owned and decorated, these one- and two-bedroom apartments have full kitchens and are luxuriously appointed with modern furnishings, stereos, and even VCRs. The small outdoor pool lacks privacy and the entire complex itself looks out over a run-down residential neighborhood and adjacent highway, but remember, you can forget all of this in the seclusion of your own apartment.

Restaurant Kissing

A PACIFIC CAFÉ, Kapaa   ◆◆◆◀
4831 Kuhio Highway (Highway 56), Suite 220
(808) 822-0013
Moderate to Expensive

Follow the Kuhio Highway north into Kapaa. The restaurant is in the Kauai Village Shopping Center, on the left.

Although A Pacific Café is considered one of the best restaurants in all of Hawaii, we were somewhat reluctant to try it when we discovered this "café" is nestled in the middle of a shopping mall, next to a shoe store. Not surprisingly, we didn't find candlelight dining for two. Instead, this stylish room is brightly lit and almost too lively for quiet conversation.

Yet the hustle and bustle seemed to disappear after our first divine bite of scallop ravioli covered in a light lime cream sauce, sprinkled with fish eggs and garnished with a beautiful array of vegetables. To our amazement, the tasting extravaganza had just begun. We oohed and aahed over angel hair pasta with Chinese pesto and grilled Hawaiian fish skewers, lobster and asparagus risotto with shrimp-tomato broth, and yellow lamb curry with brown rice, and finally concluded with a white chocolate terrine with strawberry sauce. Never mind the candles! With food like this, who needs dim lighting?

Lihue

Hotel/Bed and Breakfast Kissing

ASTON KAUAI BEACH VILLAS, Lihue
4330 Kauai Beach Drive
(808) 245-7711
Moderate

Follow Highway 56 four miles north from the airport and turn right on Kauai Beach Drive where you'll see a sign for the Outrigger Kauai Beach Villas. The Aston is on the left.

Affordable luxury is hard to come by on the east shore, where low-priced, cockroach-ridden (no kidding) hotels are in abundance. At the Aston, however, affordability and luxury go hand in hand. The ocean is just steps away from your spacious lanai in these beachfront condominiums, and the prices are so low you're bound to wonder what the catch is. There isn't one. The Aston has it all: elegant, modern furnishings, spacious one- and two-bedroom suites, tennis courts, outdoor swimming pool and Jacuzzi, and luscious white sand beach. Why can't life always be like this?

◆ **Romantic Warning:** Don't be fooled by the stately appearance of the **OUTRIGGER BEACH HOTEL,** 4331 Kauai Beach Drive, Lihue, (800) 462-6262, (Expensive to Very Expensive), which shares the Aston's idyllic location. Yes, the elegant lobby, manicured lawns, plethora of palm trees, waterfalls, and swimming pool are impressive, but the very standard hotel rooms make the Outrigger seem outrageously overpriced. Cement lanais provide pleasing beach views from your room, but this and the fact that you've left Lihue's traffic behind you are the rooms' only redeeming qualities.

Wailua

Outdoor Kissing

FERN GROTTO, Wailua

Follow the Kuhio Highway north into Wailua. Watch for signs to the Fern Grotto on your left, just past the Wailua River.

The quiet Wailua River meanders through a luxuriant tropical jungle, past tumbling waterfalls, and into the naturally formed cave amphitheater called the Fern Grotto. To fully experience the serenity and extraordinary beauty of this place, we suggest that you decline a tour with hundreds of other travelers on the Wailua River Cruise (it won't be hard to resist). Instead, be daring and rent two kayaks from **KAYAK KAUAI OUTFITTERS,** 1340 Kuhio Highway, Kapaa, (808) 822-9179, ($48 to $70 per couple). Survey this gorgeous river at your own romantic pace; why not take your time and make a day of it?

Wailua Homesteads

Hotel/Bed and Breakfast Kissing

INN PARADISE, Wailua Homesteads
6381 Makana Road
(808) 822-2542
Inexpensive to Moderate

Follow Highway 56 north and turn left onto Highway 580. Follow 580 for three miles, turn right onto Highway 581, go less than a mile, and turn right onto Opaekka Road. Take the second right onto Makana Road. The inn is the first house on the left.

You can best appreciate the beauty of Kapaa in a bed and breakfast like Inn Paradise. The modern white and gray home overlooks three acres of a lush valley, far from the madding crowd. The full wraparound lanai provides ideal vantage points for viewing the surrounding countryside and the waterfalls that sometimes emerge through the mist on the distant hillside.

Although the three available guest suites share the common lanai, all provide plenty of seclusion: private entrances, full kitchens, king- and queen-size beds, and attractive wicker and rattan furnishings. A complimentary basket filled with fruit, juice, coffee, muffins, honey, and fresh jam provides the ingredients for breakfast in bed. Linger as long as you want. There's no rush to get to the beach; it's just a quick three miles away!

ROSEWOOD BED AND BREAKFAST,
Wailua Homesteads
872 Kamalu Road
(808) 822-5216
Inexpensive to Moderate

Call for directions.

You'll breathe a sigh of relief when you leave the busy town behind and wind up into Kapaa's lush countryside. Relax in this picturesque yellow and white farmhouse framed by flowers and enclosed behind a white picket fence. You might yearn for the ocean (it's nowhere in sight) but only for a moment—the solitude and peacefulness here more than compensate for the lack of nearby water. (Besides, the beach is a mere ten minutes away.)

Two of the available guest suites in the main house are homey and spacious, but less private and appropriately less expensive. The real reason to come here is for the two self-contained cottages in the backyard. The first cottage has eclectic antique furnishings, a full kitchen, thatched roof, and private outdoor shower (popular with free spirits). We prefer the brand-new second cottage, which has a full sparkling white tiled kitchen, sun room, hardwood floors, and upstairs loft bedroom.

Discerning touches such as chocolates on your pillows and champagne for special occasions make a stay in any of the suites a pleasure. Not to mention breakfast: organic granola with macadamia nuts, fresh papaya and other tropical fruits, and Kona coffee. You'll be refreshed and ready for another blissful day in the sun.

◆ **Romantic Alternative:** If you're looking for another upcountry cabin option and don't require an ocean view, **KAY BARKER'S BED AND BREAKFAST,** Ki'inani Road, Wailua Homesteads, (808) 822-3073, (800) 835-2845, (Inexpensive), is an affordable alternative. None of the guest rooms found in the main house are worth mentioning, but the self-enclosed wood cabin in the back has real romantic potential. Enjoy views of the countryside, in addition to a small kitchenette, standard-size private bath, and fresh floral linens.

North Shore

Increased rainfall on this side of the island may be a deterrent to some, but the resulting landscape makes it a blessing in disguise. We actually found the showers invigorating, making everything extra green and fresh. The north shore also boasts some incredible beaches made famous in movies such as *South Pacific*, and the **HANALEI NATIONAL WILDLIFE RESERVE**, a fertile valley set aside for a variety of rare birds.

Haena

Outdoor Kissing

KUHIO HIGHWAY (HIGHWAY 56) ◆◆

Venture past the surprisingly busy town of Kapaa and the Kuhio Highway will take you through phenomenal surroundings. Much of the drive is waterside, but even when the ocean isn't in sight, lush foliage and dramatic rocky peaks usher you toward the north shore. The descent into the verdant **HANALEI NATIONAL WILDLIFE REFUGE** and the lookouts thereafter are the crowning glories of the drive. A narrow road, with many one-lane bridges, crosses calm rivers, leads you past two dry caves, and ends at Kee Beach, where various trails to the Na Pali Coast begin.

◆ **Romantic Warning:** Out of sheer curiosity, we drove all the way to the end of the road, which is nothing more than a busy parking lot and crowded small beach area. The two caves on the way are interesting, but unless you're starting a hike there, the finale of the highway is hardly grand and rather depressing.

KANAHA BEACH, Haena

Follow Highway 56 toward Haena and watch for signs to Charo's Restaurant on the right. The entrance to the beach is between Charo's and the Hanalei Colony Resort.

Kanaha Beach is a jewelry box full of treasures from the sea. Instead of a typical powdery beach, the sand here is made up of tiny pebbles, each one polished to smooth perfection but still distinguishable as having once been a bigger rock, living coral, or a pretty pink shell.

Swimming isn't an option due to strong currents, but the converging blue waters are incredible to watch, and the combination of shells, white coral, and unusual sand makes this a beachcomber's paradise.

◆ **Romantic Warning:** The nearby Charo's and Hanalei Colony Resort were closed for reconstruction at the time of this review. When they reopen, you may have to share this spectacular beach with crowds.

NA PALI COAST

(808) 587-0300, State Park Service
Overnight permit (free) required for backpackers

At the end of Highway 56 in Hanalei, look for signs for Na Pali Coast State Park.

One of the largest state parks in the United States, **NA PALI COAST STATE PARK** covers 6,175 spectacular acres. Heaven and earth merge at the exquisitely beautiful Na Pali coastline, a 14-mile-long rocky shoreline that is virtually inaccessible by car or foot. At the base of these formidable cliffs are some of the most remote, unspoiled beaches in the world. Verdant tropical forest and deep valleys cover the unhabitable land, making it tricky for even the most accomplished hikers and backpackers. The combination of such beauty with such difficult access is, perhaps, what keeps this domain more like heaven than earth.

Most of the area is more easily (although not intimately) seen via boat; try **LIKO KAUAI CRUISES,** (808) 338-0333, or **HANALEI SEA TOURS,** (808) 826-7254. The sea caves, lush rolling hills, mammoth cliffs, and staggering waterfalls are all breathtakingly awesome. During most boat excursions, spinner dolphins, whales, and sea turtles cavort through the waves, providing lively aquatic entertainment. Helicopter tours are also available and give you an overview of the landscape unparalleled in enchantment and beauty; try **ISLAND HELICOPTERS,** (808) 245-8588.

With the right shoes (it can get wet), athletic prowess (some of the ascents are fairly steep), and provisions (such as water and snacks), you can also hike into the region. For a single but arduous day trek, follow a four-mile round-trip trail starting from **HAENA BEACH PARK** and ending at **HANAKAPIAI BEACH.** Branching off from this path is a four-mile round-trip approach to stunning **HANAKAPIAI FALLS.** Although it takes a relatively healthy body to consummate this journey, the glimpse of Eden is phenomenal. For those who can kiss and backpack, the 11-mile (one-way) **KALALAU TRAIL** overflows with scenic wonder. (May through September, **CAPTAIN ZODIAK TOURS,** (808) 826-9371, offers drop-off and pickup service for backpackers with legal permits.) Depending on your level of expertise the hike can take two to three days.

◆ **Romantic Warning:** The waters here can be rough and rollicking, making even the most stalwart seasick. Estimate your tolerance level before you head out or this can turn out to be the boat cruise from hell.

Hanalei

Outdoor Kissing

KAYAK KAUAI OUTFITTERS, Hanalei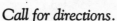
55088 Kuhio Highway (Highway 56)
(808) 826-9844
$48 to $70 per couple

Call for directions.

Kayaks can carry couples to quintessential Kauai—try to say that three times fast! The carefree staff here will strap a couple of kayaks on your car and send you on your merry way. We felt a bit unprepared but it truly was as easy as we were told, and the tranquillity we found on the Hanalei River was sublime. We wouldn't have believed the brilliant orange hau tree flowers floating on the water and fish jumping repeatedly if we hadn't seen them for ourselves.

Kissing might be difficult between kayaks, but be daring—the water is shallow in most places and warm. If you can both swim, the worst that can happen is that you'd be in the water together. Doesn't sound so bad, does it? Chances are, especially if you're beginners like us, you'll get pretty wet anyhow, so dress accordingly.

◆ **Romantic Note:** On this particular river, the first half of the journey is close to the road and breezy, but hang in there— once you go under the bridge, the waters are calmer and the scenery only gets better.

◆ **Romantic Suggestion:** Bring a sack lunch and picnic at the grassy pasture you'll find at the end of the river. **THE HANALEI GOURMET**, 5-5161 Kuhio Highway, (808) 826-2524, (Inexpensive), is close by and can pack an OK meal. The sandwich variety is good; just ask them to go light on the mayo and mustard. Our lunches were rather soggy by the time we ate, and not because we had dropped them in the river.

Kilauea

Hotel/Bed and Breakfast Kissing

PAVILIONS AT SEACLIFF, Kilauea
Reservations through Bali Hai Realty
(808) 826-7244, (808) 828-6615
Unbelievably Expensive

Call for directions.

When you drive through the stately weathered brass gates and see this property, you'll wonder "Is this really all for me?" Your significant other may remind you that it's for "us," but relax and get ready for the "complete retreat" as it has been appropriately dubbed. At the risk of sounding like the glossy brochure, this home, perched atop seven manicured acres, has everything: three ocean-view master suites, blue tiled pool and Jacuzzi, a tennis court and sand volleyball court, a charming gazebo, landscaped putting green, exercise room, full kitchen, and spacious living and dining rooms—all for your own private use! The Euro-style decor in cream and granite is tastefully elegant, and you won't believe the unobstructed vista of rolling surf and majestic mountains seen from almost every inch of the property.

◆ **Romantic Note:** There is a three-day minimum stay required here. Office facilities are available for your use, but if you can, leave work behind and devote your stay to the rare indulgences found here. The full maid, butler, and catering services available are much more conducive to romance than the business center.

◆ **Romantic Suggestion:** With all the amenities and space, sharing this home with one or two couples could still be romantic and would place this exceptional property in the Expensive price range.

Restaurant Kissing

CASA DI AMICI, Kilauea
2484 Keneke Street
(808) 828-1388
Moderate to Expensive

*Head north on Highway 56, turn right into Kilauea Town, and follow
signs for the lighthouse. Turn left onto Lighthouse Road; the restaurant
is on the right, in the Kong Lung Center.*

This charming restaurant serves absolutely delicious Italian
food. A white, lattice-framed entrance invites you into the small
open-air dining room adorned with hanging plants, rattan chairs,
and footed pedestal tables covered in crisp white linens. Soft
melodies from the piano in the center of the room fill the air, along
with the savory aroma of traditional Italian dishes.

Start your meal with a fresh salad or unusual appetizer, such as
the roasted red peppers served hot with quartered tomatoes and
anchovies in olive oil. For the main course, seafood dishes are
especially good; try the flavorful Scampi Alla Casa Di Amici—
jumbo prawns, garlic, capers, fresh tomatoes, and olive oil served
on a generous bed of linguine. Or be creative and combine your
favorite pasta with one of six rich sauces. Salsa di noci, a distinctive
walnut sauce with fresh Romano cheese, marjoram, and cream, is
sure to satisfy. Top off your meal with a foamy cappuccino and
dessert; all of them are superb.

◆   **Romantic Note:** If service had been faster and more
attentive, this place would have earned four lips. Reservations
are a must.

Princeville

Hotel/Bed and Breakfast Kissing

HALE 'AHA, Princeville
3875 Kamehameha Road
(808) 826-6733, (800) 826-6733
Moderate to Very Expensive

*Head north on Highway 56 and turn right into the Princeville Resort.
Follow the main road (Ka Haku), then turn right onto Kamehameha
Road; the house is on the right.*

You'll find this affectionate bed and breakfast nestled in the
otherwise impersonal Princeville Resort. The mix of vacation
rentals and private residences in this sprawling development can
make a tourist feel a bit like an intruder, Hale 'Aha is an intimate
alternative. Two of the three rooms in this home are well worth
recommending. The Penthouse Suite covers the entire upper
level, with a private lanai facing the ocean, king-size bed, large
sitting area, open-beamed ceilings, small kitchenette, and washer
and dryer. The Jacuzzi tub in the bathroom is big enough for two
and sits beneath Japanese lanterns. The Honeymoon Suite on the
main level is smaller but also has a big Jacuzzi tub, king-size bed,
kitchenette, small sitting area, and decent views of the ocean and
golf course.

The pastel color scheme, from white-washed beams and
floral pastel curtains down to peach carpeting, is a bit overdone.
Yet everything is clean and new, and guests have ample privacy.
Your continental breakfast is made complete with fresh home-
made bread.

HANALEI NORTH SHORE ◆◆
PROPERTIES, LTD., Princeville
P.O. Box 607
(808) 826-9622, (800) 488-3336
Expensive to Unbelievably Expensive

Call for directions.

Although the office is in Princeville, the incredible homes managed by this company are scattered along the north shore, from Haena to Moloaa Bay. These homes range from one to four bedrooms and most have views; some are even on beachfront property. Without a doubt, a private home can be a nice alternative to a busy resort or standard-issue condo. Special indulgences can include cook or maid service, even personal massages. Just be specific and define your romantic needs (as far as lodging goes, that is), and this friendly office will accommodate you.

◆ **Romantic Note:** A one-week minimum stay is required, but once you see the north shore and all it has to offer, you'll be thankful for this rule.

KALANI AINA, Princeville ◆
4620 Kuawa Road
(808) 828-1123
Inexpensive

Call for directions.

Kalani Aina has something unique to offer, but only for true animal lovers: puppies! The friendly owners of this homey bed and breakfast raise golden retrievers on the side, and even if your timing isn't right to see puppies, the puppy-parents and resident horse are lovable as well. Set in a cozy neighborhood several miles from the beach, this home offers one room with a king-size bed draped in floral linens, a small sitting area, and double-headed shower. The hammock on the deck hangs just outside your door for lazy afternoons, and the tiled hot tub sitting under a gazebo could be perfect on moonlit nights. A light English breakfast of fresh coffee and juices, fresh fruit, a variety of cereals, toast, jellies, and fresh pastries is served on the lanai.

◆ **Romantic Note:** Though the accommodations are pretty standard and dog hair is nearly impossible to avoid, seeing your honey get kisses from a fuzzy little puppy could melt your heart and hopefully inspire more kissing of your own.

Outdoor Kissing

KAWEONU BEACH

Take Highway 56 northbound and turn right into the Princeville Resort. Turn right on Kamehameha Road and follow it to the end, which is the parking lot for the Sealodge Condos. The trail to the beach begins at the oceanfront corner of the Sealodge, between two units.

Bring your sense of adventure—finding this romantic spot is half of the thrill. A bumpy overgrown dirt trail wanders down to a little stream you can easily hop over on rocks. Farther along your trek there is an imposing mass of black lava rock jutting over the water's edge. Many travelers stop here, thinking they've reached the end of the journey, but obviously those poor souls don't have our book. The secret to finding Kaweonu Beach is to not be deceived by the water on both sides of you. Continue to the left on what's left of the crumbly dirt path and be careful as you edge around the corner. When you joyfully (and finally) behold the strip of sandy beach tucked into this hidden cove, walk just a little more and give each other a pat on the back (or more if you like)—you worked hard to find this special spot.

◆ **Romantic Note:** As hard as it seems to find, this beach is not as private as we had hoped. It certainly wasn't crowded, but we would have preferred to have it all to ourselves. Who wouldn't?

◆ **Romantic Warning:** The hike isn't lengthy but the trail is a bit steep, narrow, and difficult at times. A healthy heart and shoes with good traction are a must.

Wainiha

Hotel/Bed and Breakfast Kissing

TASSA HANALEI, Wainiha   ◆◆
5121 Wainiha Powerhouse Road
(808) 826-7298
Inexpensive to Moderate

Call for directions.

New-age California meets laid-back Hawaii in this funky but charming bed and breakfast modeled after a Zen Buddhist retreat center and situated deep in the residential foothills of Hanalei. Notice the shells embedded in stepping stones as you enter, and the "Healing Temple," an all-white, open-air bungalow set aside for massages and aromatherapy. This place is unique.

Of the three lodging options, a modest cabin offers the most privacy and room, but the Queen Lily and Princess Kaiulani suites on the lower level are superior due to recent renovations. Both have French doors that open out to a river, just yards away. Beautiful furnishings, queen-size beds, rich colored carpets, stained glass windows, and lovely portraits of the Hawaiian queen and princess are all tastefully executed.

Guests are welcome to use a shared outdoor garden bathroom with gazebo and the communal hot tub and encouraged to take a swim in the river, which is really more like a gently gurgling stream.

To ensure your privacy, a scrumptious and creative breakfast is left on your doorstep. Sample home-baked sweet breads or macaroon crêpes filled with mango and topped with yogurt.

◆ **Romantic Warning:** Children are allowed and the owners have two themselves, which may discourage complete tranquillity. Then again, complete tranquillity is hard to find anywhere, with or without kids.

Hawaii
(The Big Island)

> *"A kiss is the anatomical juxtaposition of two orbicular muscles in a state of contraction."*
>
> **Cary Grant**

HAWAII—THE BIG ISLAND

When they say big, they mean big! Hawaii, the largest island in the Hawaiian archipelago, is known quite appropriately as "the Big Island," although we prefer to call it huge. The island encompasses an awesome 4,000 square miles, and thanks to continuing explosions from Kilauea, the magma-spewing volcano, it is still growing. Topographically speaking, it has a stunning assortment of unique features: snow-dabbed mountaintops (winter only), endless acres of barren black lava beds, verdant, tropical rain forests, and some of the tallest mountain peaks in the United States.

From a tourist's perspective, it is unique. In comparison to the other islands, this one has an atypical personality of its own. Beaches here are few and far between and most are primarily composed of lava rock or black sand. Although you can swim to your heart's content in these distinctive waters, the shoreline is more conducive to viewing than swimming or sunbathing. Still, the lack of sandy swimming beaches and the vast beds of encrusted lava have prevented this island oasis from becoming inundated with the horrors of commercialism (to the developers' dismay). And the developers' dilemma is a tropical lovers' delight. The snorkeling and the sunsets here are extraordinary. Plus, there are plenty of wide open spaces to be found, enough so that you never really feel the impact of civilization. The whole island has a population of 100,000, which is sparse in proportion to its size. (Oahu, at one-third the size, has 1 million people, and Maui, only slightly larger than Oahu, has 200,000.)

Driving around this island is a wondrous, but extremely long, excursion; reserve a full day (it takes at least eight hours). Mile after mile reveals a dramatic variety of landscapes. On the dry northwest side, at the base of Mauna Kea and Mauna Lani, rising an imperious 13,000 feet and 11,000 feet respectively, the boundless, rolling chaparral abruptly turns into a desolate expanse of lava field. Just beyond this bleak moonscape is the breathtaking Kohala Coast, with its magnificent but hard-to-reach shoreline. Although most of the beaches along this stretch of coast are too dangerous for swimming, they offer gorgeous vantage points for scintillating sunsets.

Farther south lies the old Hawaiian fishing village of Kailua-Kona, which has become increasingly commercialized over the last five years and is the largest tourist attraction on the Big Island. Fortunately, this is really the only place you'll find crowds on the island. To the south of this is the Gold Coast, which has exquisite snorkeling (some of the best) in many of its underwater sea parks. And to the east is the tiny two-store town (no kidding) of Volcano, as well as Hawaii Volcanoes National Park, where you can study the awesome history of the earth's creation.

Truly, this is an island of natural wonders and romantic seclusion. Thankfully, most of the island's accommodations (with the exception of those in Kailua-Kona and Hilo) are separated by many miles from each other, offering relatively undisturbed solace in the surrounding natural beauty for those seeking sanctuary from life in the fast lane.

◆ **Romantic Warning:** Hilo is the largest city on the Big Island fronting a wide expanse of ocean, but that is its only claim to fame. The accommodations here leave much to be desired and the town is run-down. Accessible nearby beaches are limited, and the few there are have become tent cities for the homeless. Hilo has a couple of intriguing restaurants (see Hilo's "Restaurant Kissing" section) and **BANYAN TREE DRIVE** is beautiful, but that's really about it.

◆ **Romantic Note:** Pure Kona coffee is the most flavorful in the world. There is nothing else quite so smooth and rich. Coffee lovers should by all means imbibe this magic brew to see why the gods still choose the Big Island as a place to indulge their eccentricities. Be cautious; not everyone serves pure Kona coffee. Some places use a blend of beans, containing as little as 10 to 20 percent Kona, and with nowhere the same taste as unadulterated Kona. Insist on the real thing.

Kailua-Kona

The town of Kailua-Kona is approximately 15 minutes south of the Keohole Airport on Highway 11.

Kailua-Kona is the Big Island's largest tourist stopover, and its shores, nearby streets, and highways are bursting at the seams with hotels, restaurants, cafés, gift stores, gas stations, and local residences. This is a bit startling once you have seen the rest of the Big Island, because you can go for miles before you'll see civilization like this again. Although the crowds in Kailua-Kona hardly compare to those in Waikiki on the island of Oahu (thank goodness), be forewarned that this is not the place to come for quiet refuge on great beaches. Nevertheless, Kailua-Kona welcomes you in warm Hawaiian style, offering many options for tourists who seek easily accessible lodging, dining, and entertainment.

Hotel/Bed and Breakfast Kissing

ASTON ROYAL SEA CLIFF RESORT,
Kailua-Kona
75-6040 Alii Drive
(808) 329-8021
Moderate to Expensive

Head south on Alii Drive from the town of Kailua-Kona. The resort is several miles down on the right.

You might feel like you've walked right into a postcard as you enter this terraced, white stucco condominium resort overlooking the turquoise blue sea, framed by swaying palm trees. But this is much better than a picture! You can actually feel the spray of the violent Pacific surf as it thunders against the black lava rock beach, which the hotel fronts.

Although the white stucco could use some touching up, the Aston's unique design is a welcome change from the repetitious, nondescript, and considerably run-down hotels throughout Kailua-

Kona. Stroll through white, spacious open-air hallways to your elegant one- or two-bedroom suite; their refined decor includes view lanais, cushioned wicker furnishings, modern art, soothing pastels, large tiled baths, and beautifully patterned linens. Fortunately, you don't have to pay exorbitant prices for splendor. As the rooms get larger and the views get more spectacular, so do the prices, but even the smaller, less expensive suites offer luxurious decor and lovely garden or partial ocean views.

You don't have to leave your room for sunset. Just throw open the door to your private lanai and behold the exhilarating arrival of dusk (it's a different painting every night) as the sun brushes the canvas where the ocean meets the sky. Look long enough at the sun and you might even catch a glimpse of the infamous "green flash" (known to happen just as the sun sets).

Last but not least, two outdoor pools have unobstructed ocean views and are surrounded by a well-groomed landscape with colorful flower beds, a small waterfall, palm trees, and an expansive lush lawn. When dusk's cool breezes arrive, refresh yourselves in the surf and then warm yourselves in the Jacuzzi. Luxury should always be this affordable!

HALE MALIA BED AND BREAKFAST, Kailua-Kona
(808) 326-1641
Inexpensive

Call for address and directions.

What a find! A contemporary, oceanfront home, highlighted by a wraparound lanai that is only a few yards away from the crashing Pacific surf. You can take in the lava rock beach and dazzling ocean views from a window seat in the capacious common room, graced with square white pillars, white-washed beams, a cathedral ceiling, and casual decor. Or whale watch from a hammock on the small private beach, filled with more volcanic debris and not accessible for swimming, in the front yard.

The two guest rooms are somewhat homespun, yet both offer adequate comfort and private baths, one of which is down the hall.

Our favorite was the room facing out toward the lanai and the ocean beyond, awash in sunlight and exuding a pleasant country charm. The second guest room is, unfortunately, much less desirable. Although it faces the garden and has a partial ocean view (if you can call it that), it offers considerably less light and the decor is somewhat lackluster.

In the morning a hearty continental breakfast of fruits, fresh-baked muffins, and Kona coffee is served on the lanai as a prelude to an active day of snorkeling, fishing, kayaking, scuba diving, or sight-seeing, all just minutes away in the town of Kailua-Kona.

KAILUA PLANTATION HOUSE, Kailua-Kona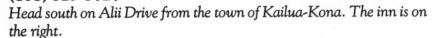
75-5948 Alii Drive
(808) 329-3727
Head south on Alii Drive from the town of Kailua-Kona. The inn is on the right.

Ah, sanctuary at last. Many of the Big Island's bed and breakfasts are private homes that have been converted to accommodate guests; more often than not they are too casual (like visiting a retired relative) for comfort. But the Plantation House is a welcome exception to this rule and redefines the concept of bed and breakfast in Hawaii. Built and designed to serve exclusively as a bed and breakfast, this inn offers its guests the intimacy and seclusion of a bed and breakfast with the luxury of a superior hotel. A rare combination, especially in the Hawaiian Islands.

The impressive and newly built two-story mansion is perched atop a black lava beach, offering exquisite views of the turbulent Pacific surf from every angle. The only potential drawback to its location is the busy street behind the house, but luckily the inn's design is such that you don't even know the traffic is there once you're inside. You can relish the ocean breezes undisturbed from the spacious and stylish common room, wraparound lanai, outdoor Jacuzzi, or small triangular dipping pool. And you've only just begun.

All of the five guest rooms have spectacular ocean views, private baths and lanais, and enticing details. The deluxe first-floor suite, done in blue tones with plush, attractive linens, offers a platform Jacuzzi tub for two, accentuated by an overhead skylight. The Kai o Lani ("Heavenly Waters") Room boasts an equally captivating ocean view, as well as a bamboo and rattan queen-size canopy bed and spacious bathroom with Jacuzzi tub. Even the smaller African-style room is seductive with its zebra prints, burgundy tones, and rattan and bamboo furnishings. You just can't go wrong. You feel pampered from the moment you arrive, and the morning's full buffet breakfast of fresh-baked muffins, breads, baked dishes, local fruits, and Kona coffee only makes your departure that much more difficult. In that case, you might just want to book another night.

KONA HILTON, Kailua-Kona   ❧
75-5852 Alii Drive
(808) 329-3111
Moderate to Expensive

Follow Alii Drive south from Kailua-Kona. The Hilton is several miles down on the right.

At first glance, the Hilton's three colossal white terraced buildings are out of place on this rugged tropical beachfront. It is hard to believe there are only 444 rooms here, because it feels more like a thousand. You shouldn't come here looking for quiet moments, but the brochure leads you to think otherwise, boasting of tourist delights such as a private lagoon, freshwater swimming pool, coconut grove, and lovely ocean views. If the hotel were more secluded and had a better floor plan, romantics undoubtedly *would* be delighted by these tropical amenities. However, because of its vast size and busy location (directly off highly trafficked Alii Drive), the Hilton is not for everybody.

This overwhelming hotel complex offers everything (except peace and quiet): tennis courts, nearby golf courses, shopping, oceanfront restaurants, moderately priced (and fairly attractive) hotel rooms with cement lanais that have decent views, and close proximity to Kailua-Kona's various tourist activities.

You can count on the Hilton to provide affordable essentials, but don't count on the surroundings to cultivate romance. The Hilton leaves that entirely up to you. So why are we including it? Its convenient location (a perfect stopover on your way to other areas on the island), reasonable price, and amenities are ideal for tourists with smaller budgets whose idea of romance is being on the move.

MERRYMAN'S BED AND BREAKFAST, Kealakekua
(808) 323-2276
Inexpensive

Call for address and directions.

You can witness all the tropics has to offer in this large and inviting two-story cream and white farmhouse set on a breezy hillside with distant, panoramic views of the Kona Coast. The exposed beams, cathedral ceiling, and hardwood tiled floor in the sizable upstairs living room create a unique, country atmosphere. Unwind in the cozy comfort of cushioned wicker furnishings while looking out the sweeping bay windows that focus attention on the sparkling ocean beyond. And that's just the common area.

The homey Deluxe Master Suite features beautiful linens, a private all-wood bathroom, a lanai, and a limited ocean view. A brand-new downstairs guest room, replete with pastel floral linens, sparkling tiled bath, and private entrance, is perfect for couples who desire more privacy. The remaining two upstairs guest rooms share a bath (which is large, but obviously not private) and offer sufficient elbow room.

Your hosts don't attempt to compete with the ocean (a ten-minute drive away). They simply offer you all the comforts of their sunny home, including a plentiful continental breakfast. For those who want to lounge around the countryside or explore the Kona Gold Coast and don't need the beach out the front door, this is an ideal retreat.

◆ **Romantic Note: KEALAKEKUA BAY** is ten minutes from Merryman's, and the drive itself is well worth every splendid moment. Wind down a lushly tropical residential hillside past coconut and papaya trees, exotic flowers, and warbling colorful birds. The mesmerizing blue Pacific expands below you and beckons you closer at every turn. Unfortunately, when you finally reach the water's edge, you're apt to find a crowd of locals and tourists waiting to snorkel in the underwater sealife park. The snorkeling is wonderful, but you're better off snorkeling elsewhere with fewer people. So turn around and delight in the gorgeous drive once more, this time on the way back up.

THE SEA VILLAGE CONDOMINIUM, Kailua-Kona ◆◀
75-6002 Alii Drive
(808) 538-7145
Inexpensive to Moderate

Head south on Alii Drive from Kailua-Kona. The condominium is several miles down on the right.

Looking for a change of pace? Condominium rentals can be affordable alternatives for those with smaller budgets who seek romantic asylum on the Big Island. Condominiums don't provide the intimate service of a bed and breakfast or the sumptuous surroundings of a luxury hotel, but the Sea Village does provide ample one- or two-bedroom fully equipped apartments with unhindered privacy for extremely reasonable prices. (It actually feels like a steal.)

Extend your vacation in paradise here (a three-day minimum is required) and relax in the comfort of your own apartment. Choose from garden-view, ocean-view, or oceanfront suites (the better the view, the higher the price), each with a fully furnished kitchen, washer and dryer, view lanai, and weekly maid service. The decor is pleasant, although standard, but your privacy is optimum. Lounge near the small oceanside pool and sip a drink from the convenient wet bar, or be daring and embark together from the lava rock beach into the frenzied Pacific surf, literally yards away.

And for those who like to be near the center of action, Kailua-Kona's restaurants, shopping, snorkeling, and tourist activities are a five-minute drive away.

Restaurant Kissing

KONA INN RESTAURANT, Kailua-Kona   ❤❤
75-5744 Alii Drive
(808) 329-4455
Inexpensive to Moderate

In the heart of Kailua-Kona at the Fisherman's Wharf. Follow Alii Drive through Kailua; the Wharf is on the left.

Many tourists have been known to take refuge from the commotion of Kailua-Kona in a high-backed wicker chair with a cool drink in hand, gazing out over the Pacific, at the Kona Inn. This elegant but casual oceanfront restaurant nestled in the midst of a charming stretch of shops provides the perfect sojourn for weary and hungry tourists. Walk through etched glass doors into the open-air dining room graced with Oriental throw rugs and cozy wood tables with ocean views. The tables are somewhat crowded together, so request one nearest to the bulkhead and expect to get close. (You can never get too close to the one you love).

Don't expect too much from the menu, which offers a standard selection of mostly seafood, ranging from jumbo fried shrimp to steak and lobster. Still, the wait staff is pleasant and prices are more than reasonable. Not to mention the ocean surf, practically lapping at your feet.

◆ **Romantic Alternative: FISHERMAN LANDING,** 75-5744 Alii Drive, Kailua-Kona, (808) 326-2555, (Inexpensive), is another option for tourists who want to put up their feet and drink in views of the ocean. Just a few steps down the wharf from the Kona Inn, you can enjoy the waves breaking over black lava rocks in a more casual setting. Green umbrellas shade tables on a wooden deck framed by wood pillars, while hanging lanterns and mounted sharks create a rustic ambience in the open-air dining room. Entrées here are less expensive and even more basic, but adequate. After a cocktail and a chicken or fish sandwich, walk hand-in-hand down the weathered brick promenade and marvel at the awesome power of the open sea.

PALM CAFÉ, Kailua-Kona
75-5819 Alii Drive
(808) 329-7128
Moderate

Drive south on Alii Drive from the town of Kailua-Kona and turn left at the Coconut Grove Marketplace.

Appropriately, palm trees encircle the two-story building that houses this lovely second-floor open-air café overlooking the street below and the ocean beyond. White French doors open into a commodious dining room, and an abundance of plants, floral fabrics, booths with colorful pillows, and wood and wicker furnishings entice you to stay. Sadly, the never-ceasing traffic of Alii Drive below, which separates the restaurant from the beach, detracts from the café's charming ambience.

Even so, this is one of Kailua-Kona's more romantic and innovative dining options. Relish the flavor of fresh Hawaiian fish grilled with ginger, green onion, shoyu, and hot peanut oil, or the oven-baked ono with a remarkable almond-sesame crust. Papaya-tomato relish caresses steamed salmon with sweet Kona onion confit and shiitake mushrooms in a won bok cabbage pocket. The kitchen deftly handles the Pacific Rim cuisine accented with French-Asian flavors, which is sure to please even the pickiest palates, despite the outside traffic.

PHILLIP PAOLO'S, Kailua-Kona
Waterfront Row #2
(808) 329-4436
Moderate to Expensive

Follow Alii Drive several miles south from the town of Kailua-Kona to Waterfront Row, a wooden shopping center and restaurant complex on the right. Phillip Paolo's is on the second floor.

Your romantic inclinations will be well tended in the posh surroundings of this Italian restaurant nestled in the second floor of a charming, natural-wood shopping center. Open beams and high ceilings with skylight windows soar above snug booths highlighted with swirls of rolled fabric, candles, pink and green linens, and paintings of Italian cityscapes. Distant views of the ocean and palm trees remind you that you are in the tropics, but the ambrosial aromas take you halfway around the world.

Although the food is excellent, the menu is fairly limited, offering a small selection of Italian dishes, with an emphasis on pasta and chicken. Sample fettuccine with crabmeat, creamy garlic butter, and onions, or pasta crêpes filled with chopped fresh spinach and ricotta cheese. Despite the menu's limitations and lack of variety, the food is rumored to be some of the best on the Big Island. In fact, the combination of delicious food and delightful ambience could lead to some delirious kisses.

Holualoa

Hotel/Bed and Breakfast Kissing

HOLUALOA INN, Holuloa
(808) 324-1121
Inexpensive to Moderate

Call for address and directions.

Colorful meetings of Eastern, Western, and Polynesian cultures, traditions, people, and cuisine are a hallmark of the Hawaiian Islands. The Holualoa Inn honors this ideal by deriving its bucolic elegance from sources around the world. The three-story cedar inn stretches gracefully atop the upper portion of a 40-acre working cattle ranch and coffee farm. Enfolded by fig, papaya, and plumeria trees, you can lose yourself in enchanting views of the surrounding countryside, Kailua Bay, and the Pacific beyond.

The inn itself is reminiscent of the mainland's Pacific Northwest. Cedar walls, exposed beams, and cathedral ceilings blend harmoniously with polished eucalyptus floors that extend throughout the rambling house. You'll find ample space for two in the expansive upstairs and downstairs common areas, which are tastefully (though sparsely) appointed with unusual, contemporary art pieces and a mixture of modern and antique furnishings. A grand piano and a billiard table provide options for entertainment (not that you'd need them for romance), and a small kitchenette stocked with complimentary snacks is available for guests at all hours. Borrow a book from the lending library and curl up in one of innumerable cozy corners. Better yet, luxuriate near the outdoor pool in a lounge chair and bask in the sunshine.

Choose from four alluring guest rooms (they really are amazing) with authentic Polynesian themes. The rooms are scattered throughout the house so that each offers the utmost privacy. Unique wooden beds, fascinating art, sizable baths (one room has a Jacuzzi tub), ocean views, and beautiful floral linens invite you to stay inside. But before you do, steal to the rooftop gazebo for the best ocean views and a starlight kiss.

Wait, it's not over yet. Awaken to streaming sunlight and the aromas of a home-cooked breakfast. Sample local fruits and relish the host's custard French toast, waffles, or cheese breakfast casserole. We're not exaggerating—this one is as romantic as it gets.

Kohala Coast

Barren yet breathtaking, the seemingly eternal stretches of black lava end abruptly at the thundering Pacific surf in a surrealistic natural landscape. The unrelenting beds of lava and the absence of sandy swimming beaches have deterred hotel development here (and elsewhere on the island), so relatively little of the land is marred by cement and steel. Consequently, the existing resorts along the Kohala Coast are exceedingly secluded. Plan to make yourselves at home in the resort of your choice, because there is little in terms of restaurants and shopping anywhere nearby. But who needs shopping? You will have everything you need, and more, in the confines of your hotel and in the surrounding visual splendor of nearby mountains and water. If you crave privacy more than you crave swimming and sand, the Kohala Coast is your slice of heaven.

Hotel/Bed and Breakfast Kissing

HALE WAILEA, Kohala Coast
Reservations through Hawaii's Best Bed and Breakfast
(808) 885-4550, (800) 262-9912
Moderate

Call for directions

Enjoy a tropical dream come true—your own private home at the beach in Hawaii. Well, it isn't right on the beach, but if across the street is good enough, this comfortable, modest home with a spacious deck is a reasonably priced facsimile of most people's favorite Hawaiian fantasy. Cane furniture, hardwood floors, sliding glass doors that open to the ocean, a small but well-equipped kitchen stocked with breakfast provisions, a fireplace, and two bedrooms with windows all around add up to a private Hawaiian escape. Soak up the scenery, sit back, hold hands, and breathe in the relaxation.

KONA VILLAGE, Kailua-Kona
(808) 325-5555, (800) 367-5290
Expensive to Very Expensive

Six miles north of Keahole Airport on Highway 11, on the left. It's easy to miss, so look for a cluster of flagpoles and a small wooden tollbooth.

This is an escapist's dream, but you *really* have to be in the mood to leave it all behind in order to luxuriate in this blissful retreat. Sneak away to the isolation of an ancient seaside Hawaiian fishing village and sleep under a thatched roof in a private, self-contained *hale* (bungalow) designed exclusively for romantic exile. Leave your schedules at home, because there isn't a trace of the real world here. No cars, televisions, telephones, alarm clocks, or radios are to be found on the premises. Even room service can take a full day to fulfill your requests. Those who can't live without today's modern conveniences would be better off elsewhere, but those who want to experience togetherness without distractions might never want to leave this one-of-a-kind tropical oasis.

More than 100 hales, done in a variety of authentic tasteful and colorful Polynesian themes (Samoan, Fijian, Tahitian, and more) are scattered across 82 acres of tropical oceanfront property. Although furnishings in the hales are simple, they include all the required comforts: king-size beds, attractive linens, private baths, and a refrigerator (for a charge). Dusty walking paths meander past bungalows tucked under palm trees, nestled near a large lagoon teeming with birds, or scattered along a stretch of natural sandy beach. It feels magical after dark as you walk beneath the sky's arena of twinkling stars or listen to the gentle rush of the man-made waterfall from the spacious outdoor hot tub or small swimming pool (there are two on the property).

Civilization feels light-years away, and this aura is enhanced by the fact that you don't have to worry about money (until you pay the tab, of course). Experience a cashless society where three daily meals are provided and included in the room price. So what's the catch? Although their weekly luau is renowned as one of the best on the Big Island, be forewarned that the food at both of the restaurants here is mediocre to poor. What a disappointment in an otherwise idyllic romantic find.

MAUNA LANI BAY HOTEL
AND BUNGALOWS, Kohala Coast
1 Mauna Lani Drive
(808) 885-6622, (800) 367-2323
Very Expensive to Beyond Unbelievably Expensive

From the Keahole Airport, follow Highway 11 north. Watch for signs; the entrance to the hotel is on the left.

When *Lifestyles of the Rich and Famous* rated the Mauna Lani Bay the number-one resort in the United States, they were probably referring to the five unique, ultra-luxurious bungalows that only the rich and famous could possibly afford. The hotel is set on the rugged and secluded Kohala Coast, surrounded by a premier waterfront golf course etched in black lava rock, lush foliage, manicured grounds, waterfalls, and protected fishponds. But those bungalows (ten lips at least!) are located right on the water's edge, with panoramic ocean views. Each one has more space then most homes, including a sumptuous marble bath, Jacuzzi, private pool, personal butler, and plush oversized furnishings, all for about $2,500 a night. If you can swallow the price you already know about overindulging the senses.

For the rest of us, the five-story open-air lobby hints of older construction, but recent renovations added a fresh welcoming grandeur. The guest rooms have also undergone refurbishment and are attractive and exceedingly comfortable, though somewhat on the snug side. Most have lanais that look out to the spectacular ocean view, helping to create a more spacious feeling inside. Resort amenities abound, starting with the aforementioned championship golf course (you've probably seen it on TV, with its unparalleled over-the-water par-three hole), tennis courts, lovely swimming pool, white sand beach, health club, and six restaurants, including **THE CANOE HOUSE** (reviewed elsewhere in this section).

◆ **Romantic Note: THE OCEAN VILLAS** at the Mauna Lani Bay are a nice compromise between the less extravagant but affordable hotel rooms and the ultra-plush and outrageously expensive bungalows. The villas have full-size kitchens, ocean views, and separate living and dining areas. Located nearby but owned by a different company, **MAUNA LANI POINT**, 50 Nohea Kai Drive, Lahaina, (808) 667-1400, (800) 642-6284, (Expensive), is yet another luxury condominium resort. The elegant and roomy one-, two- and three-bedroom suites feature views of the golf course and ocean. These hardly compare to the bungalows at the Mauna Lani Bay Hotel, but at least the privacy here is affordable!

RITZ-CARLTON MAUNA LANI, Kohala Coast ◆◆◆◆
One North Kaniku Drive
(808) 885-2000
Very Expensive and Beyond

From the Keahole Airport, drive to Highway 11 and turn left. Follow the highway for approximately 15 miles. The hotel entrance is on the left; follow the signs.

In some ways this is just another Ritz-Carlton, but that is saying a lot about the kind of quality and refinement you can expect. As you cross the threshold into the impressive lobby, service and luxury become paramount. A winding maze of stately corridors is graced with hand-painted vases, Oriental carpets, antique furnishings, classical art, and floral wall coverings. Everything is appropriately grand yet understated. Even the elevators are replete with wood paneling, Oriental throw rugs, and overhead chandeliers. The guest suites are less ornate but do provide rich color schemes, plush linens, attractive marble baths with separate tubs and showers, and private lanais, most with arousing views of the surrounding grounds and ocean. For an extra charge, luxuriate in a Club Floor Suite, where you wake to a generous continental breakfast and douse your sweet tooth before bedtime with a late-night chocolate and cordial, served just down the hall in the elegant common room.

It only gets better from here. Traverse the 32 acres of verdant, tropical garden and golf course that encompass the sprawling hotel. Rocky waterfalls, fish ponds filled with trout, footbridges, and lush vegetation enfold you as you wind along paths past a large swimming pool with water-spitting stone frog fountains. One negative: there are only two hot tubs for more than 500 rooms. One is set near a waterfall and the other is just yards from the pounding surf, which means you sometimes (if not always) have to wait in line or sit shoulder to shoulder with strangers. If that's the case, wander farther away toward the white sandy beach and private lagoon, which is often entirely yours after dark.

◆ **Romantic Note:** You don't have to leave the property for fine dining (which is lucky because the nearest town is half an hour away). The casual poolside **CAFÉ RESTAURANT AND LOUNGE** offers a variety of healthful Pacific Rim dishes and refreshments to enjoy during breaks from swimming or sunbathing. **THE DINING ROOM** (reviewed elsewhere in this section) and **THE GRILL** will appease your appetites in first-class surroundings.

Restaurant Kissing

THE CANOE HOUSE, Kohala Coast   ◆◆◆◆
1 Mauna Lani Drive, at the Mauna Lani Bay Resort
(808) 885-6622, (800) 367-2323
Very Expensive

From the Keahole Airport, follow Highway 11 north. Watch for signs; the entrance to the hotel is on the left.

Considered one of the best restaurants on the coast, The Canoe House restaurant comes awfully close to living up to that challenging reputation. Open-air dining just beyond water's edge makes the setting alone intoxicating. The entire front length of the dining room has sliding glass doors that beautifully allow the outside to become an integral part of the inside. Wood detailing, soft lighting, comfortable seating, and responsive service fill the interior with a subtle elegance that blends perfectly with the energy of the waves and warmth of the air.

Like many of Hawaii's restaurants, The Canoe House serves Pacific Rim cuisine with a touch of continental fare thrown in to round out the menu. Presentation and fresh ingredients are emphasized here, but taste is master and everything is flavorful and delectable. Portions can be on the small side, but that can be forgiven with every savory bite.

THE DINING ROOM, Kohala Coast ◆◆◆◆
One North Kaniku Drive, at the Ritz-Carlton Mauna Lani
(808) 885-2000
Very Expensive

From the Keahole Airport, drive to Highway 11 and turn left. Follow the highway for approximately 15 miles. The hotel entrance is on the left; follow the signs.

Handsome wood paneling; distant water views; beautiful linens; formal place settings shining with silver, crystal, and china; and, most notable, flawless service. As lovely as that all sounds, it wouldn't count for much if the food wasn't some of the most innovative and delicious we've had in all of the Hawaiian Islands. Savor perfectly prepared fresh island fish, either broiled, sautéed, or grilled, with asparagus, capers, and olive vinaigrette; saffron herb sauce; or banana curry and ti-leaf-wrapped banana, among other unique choices. And dessert will make you blush with the sweetness of the moment. Every detail makes this an indulgent, ecstatic dining experience.

◆ **Romantic Note:** Best of all, in The Dining Room's lounge, you can sway arm-in-arm to live soft jazz late into the night, performed by an exceptionally talented local musician.

Waikoloa

Hotel/Bed and Breakfast Kissing

HYATT REGENCY, Waikoloa
Waikoloa Beach Resort
(808) 885-1234
Expensive to Unbelievably Expensive and Beyond

From the Keahole Airport, head north on Highway 11 for approximately 30 miles. The entrance to the Hyatt Regency is on the left; follow signs to the hotel.

Sixty-two oceanfront acres (but, alas, no natural beach) envelop this palatial wonderland, which includes 3 swimming pools, 8 restaurants, 12 lounges, 1,241 guest rooms, meeting facilities, a lagoon, a golf course, several twisting water slides, shopping, a health spa, dolphins, and more.

So how do you make your way across this gargantuan property without a map? It's easy! Hop on a ferryboat that winds through the connecting waterways, or get whisked to your destination in an electric tram. Either option can be delightful once or twice, but both grow tiresome, especially when there are crowds. So set out on foot instead and wander (for a lengthy distance) along the flagstone walkways that meander past stunning Oriental and Pacific art pieces gracing this Polynesian palace. Although there are acres upon acres of property like this to explore, most of it is man-made (waterfalls and lagoon included), and you'll find yourself longing for open stretches of untouched beach and sky. (Isn't that why you came to Hawaii?) To satisfy your cravings, you can take a shuttle bus from the hotel to the public beach next door.

Once you've found your suite, you can bask in stately (although pricey) comfort with ocean views. The Club Bay Suites are especially luxuriant, with Oriental motifs, unusual pottery, magnificent view lanais, queen-size koa wood beds, marble baths, and Jacuzzis. The Regency Club Suites include exemplary concierge service, breakfast and the morning paper, and evening cocktails with hors d'oeuvres. If your budget can handle it and you're in the mood for lots of outdoor recreation, this is heaven. Otherwise, keep moving.

◆ **Romantic Note:** The Hyatt has eight different restaurants to choose from, all just a ferryboat (or tram) ride away. One of our favorites was **DONATONI'S**, (808) 885-2893, (Expensive), located in an elegant house overlooking the waterway. The northern Italian cuisine ranges from antipasto to gourmet pizzas to veal. Another favorite is **CASCADES**, (808) 885-2888, (Moderate), an open-air dining room set beside a plunging waterfall. Select from delectable baked goods, fruits, and traditional American and Japanese dishes served at deluxe breakfast and dinner buffets. A third option is **IMARI,** (808) 885-2894, (Moderate), offering innovative Japanese cuisine and a sushi bar in a tea garden highlighted by more waterfalls.

Kawaihae

Hotel/Bed and Breakfast

MAKAI HALE, Kawaihae   ◆◆
Reservations through Hawaii's Best Bed and Breakfast
(808) 885-4550, (800) 262-9912
Inexpensive to Moderate

Call for directions.

As you wind up the hillside toward Makai Hale, the stunning splendor of the Kohala Coast becomes more apparent. Across the expanse of horizon, the crystal blue Pacific dazzles your eyes while the mountain peaks of Mona Lani and Mona Kea rise majestically to meet the sky. The vast black lava beds below stretch for what seems an eternity and then drop suddenly into the raging sea. Makai Hale takes full advantage of this view, and guests can partake in the heavenly surroundings in a self-enclosed two-bedroom suite with floor-to-ceiling windows and private lanai.

To fully embrace views of Kohala, slip out the sliding glass door of your suite onto a sweeping cement deck with a large swimming pool, Jacuzzi, and picnic tables. Sunlight fills the comfortable suite in the daytime, and the cathedral ceiling and unhindered views provide plentiful space. As wonderful as this sounds, what is lacking is style, although the view more than compensates for the plain interior, sparse furnishings, and a bathroom that leaves much to be desired. It is, however, clean—and exclusively yours. Provisions for breakfast are left in the small kitchenette by the hosts, who attempt to leave your privacy undisturbed and live in the adjacent house.

Waimea

Up here, at 2,200 feet above sea level, the days are hot, with cool breezes that blow through gently swaying trees and over idyllic lush green pastureland. The ocean is only eight miles away, but another world exists at this elevation and it is worth discovering for yourselves. Waimea is a thriving, quiet country town, home to 8,000 islanders. There are only a handful of restaurants and shops, but acres and acres of visual enchantment. For well over a hundred years the pivotal business of the region has been the **PARKER RANCH,** (808) 885-7311, the largest family-owned ranch in the United States. Currently, more than 225,000 acres are in a charitable trust serving the town of Waimea, but it began as a two-acre land grant back in 1837 from King Kamehameha I to John P. Parker. Two museums, including the owners' ranch house, are available for tours. Both provide a considerable historical retrospective.

Other than a day visit through this distinguished countryside, you should consider a loving stay. It isn't the tropical Hawaii you usually think of, but it also isn't as crowded or as expensive as the coastal areas.

◆**Romantic Note:** The last owner of the Parker Ranch, Richard Smart, died in 1991, and the will is presently being contested by the two surviving sons and three grandchildren. For now the estate remains in a charitable trust, but only time and the courts will tell what will happen to the $450 million worth of prime real estate (now home to livestock) and personal assets.

Hotel/Bed and Breakfast Kissing

PUU MANU COTTAGE, Waimea   ◆◆◆
Reservations through Hawaii's Best Bed and Breakfast
(808) 885-4550, (800) 262-9912
Inexpensive

Call for directions.

What a remarkable little hideaway. Nestled in the middle of a vast rolling meadow dotted with Rousseau-like clusters of trees at the foothills of Mauna Kea is an affectionately decorated cottage. Unbelievably, this immaculate, meticulously refurbished place was once the barn for the nearby country home of the owners. Now it is a cozy respite for those who want secluded country life and the warm Hawaiian sun. French doors that open onto a wide deck, a charming living room warmed at night by a glowing fireplace, two genial bedrooms, and a handsome open kitchen supplied with a generous morning meal are all part of the tranquil, serene indulgences you can enjoy here. Yes, the beach is a 25-minute drive away, but you get to come back to your mountain hideaway, so it doesn't really matter.

WAIKIKI COTTAGE, Waimea   💋💋
Reservations through Hawaii's Best Bed and Breakfast
(808) 885-4550, (800) 262-9912
Inexpensive

Call for directions.

Just off Saddle Road, on the slopes of Mauna Kea, framed by pristine countryside, lies Waikiki Cottage. Located 12 miles from the heart of Waimea, it is more a modest suburban home than a cottage. A delightful interior with plenty of space, vaulted wood ceilings, casual furnishings, and a well-stocked kitchen effect a homey appearance. It isn't fancy, but it is extremely cozy, and far away from the madding crowd.

◆ **Romantic Warning:** Blocking the wonderful pastoral view from the entrance is a run-down barn. It isn't a pretty picture, but there are other viewpoints that are.

WAIMEA GARDENS COTTAGE, Waimea   💋💋💋💋
Reservations through Hawaii's Best Bed and Breakfast
(808) 885-4550, (800) 262-9912,
Inexpensive

Call for directions.

As you've thumbed through the selections of bed and breakfasts in this guide, you probably have noticed references to Hawaii's Best Bed and Breakfast reservation service. Well, the owners of that select business have create a "best" bed and breakfast of their own. An impeccably renovated duplex cottage adjacent to the main house holds two lovingly decorated units bordered by a rushing creek, forest, sweeping lawn, and well-maintained English garden. The red shingled exterior is punctuated by forest green frames and a picket fence. The interiors are flawless, with marble wood-burning fireplaces, hardwood floors, alcove bedrooms, down comforters, charming kitchens, stereos, and TVs. Every detail has been attended to, so all you have to do is snuggle together and enjoy.

◆ **Romantic Note:** There is one minor drawback: the main road is too nearby for an optimum country visit. But everything else is above par and radiates warmth and comfort.

Restaurant Kissing

MERRIMAN'S RESTAURANT, Waimea
Highway 19 and Opelo Road
(808) 885-6822
Moderate to Expensive

Just off Route 19 in the heart of Waimea, in the small Opelo Plaza.

Having a reputation as one of the finest restaurants on the island is not an easy distinction to live up to. It is to the credit of the owner (whom the restaurant is named after) that the daily procession of food is truly excellent. Lunches are reliably good, but night is when the unique style of the chef takes flight. An open kitchen fronts an informal dining room with a slightly strange black, pink, and green motif. Some of the chairs are stained and the potted palm trees could use some water, but the food is so good it is easy after a few moments to ignore the interior. Our wok-charred ahi was perfectly done; the fresh catch of the day sautéed in a sesame crust and topped with a mango-lime sauce was outstanding. Fresh local meats are savory and masterfully prepared. The filet mignon in brandy cream sauce is superb.

The emphasis here is on the food, as it should be. You can save the kissing until you get home, full and satisfied from a delightful meal.

Waipio

Hotel/Bed and Breakfast Kissing

HALE WAIPIO, Waipio   ◆ ◆ ◆
Reservations through Hawaii's Best Bed and Breakfast
(808) 885-4550, (800) 262-9912
Moderate

Call for directions.

Sea cliffs loom over a rolling green hill, the endless ocean lies before you, and there are no neighbors in sight for as far as the eye can see. Here you are in a stunning, specially designed country home complete with an ample wraparound deck, a cozy fireplace, tall ceilings, a well-supplied kitchen (breakfast fixings included), and all the privacy you could ask for. There is no nearby beach, but the sheer beauty and total seclusion of the spot make it an impeccable hideaway for two.

◆ **Romantic Note:** The spectacular **WAIPIO VALLEY** (reviewed elsewhere in this section) is only a few minutes away from the home.

Outdoor Kissing

WAIPIO VALLEY, Waipio   ◆ ◆ ◆ ◆
Waipio Valley Shuttle, (808) 775-7121
Waipio Valley Wagon Tours, (808) 775-9518
Between $25 to $35 per person for a one-and-a-half-hour tour.

Call for directions.

An excursion through the Waipio Valley is a passage to gorgeous tropical vegetation, cascading waterfalls, and breathtaking cliffs that end abruptly at water's edge. It is also a journey through history. King Kamehameha I established his long reign over the islands from this location. Formidable battles, human sacrifices, and peaceful agriculture were all part of life in this mesmerizing valley. Hawaii's past seems very alive here—take a moment to contemplate the ancient stories these sands could tell.

◆ **Romantic Note:** If you are interested in a more intimate trek and are also capable of handling a fairly steep ascent out of the valley (going in is downhill, so that part is easy), hiking is a definite option. Watertight shoes are a necessity, as is a backpack and light rain gear. This is the rainy part of the island.

Volcano

Don't be surprised if you awaken to a small earthquake in the middle of the night. Rumbling earth (among other things, like a lava flow closing down sections of roadway) is just an accepted part of life in Volcano. The tiny two-store town ("town" actually feels like a misnomer; "village" or "neighborhood" might be better) has a bevy of bed and breakfasts. Everything in Volcano is just minutes away from **HAWAII VOLCANOES NATIONAL PARK,** the area's only real attraction. Kilauea, the unpredictable volcano, continues its eruptive activity with majestic but frustrating glory. A recent lava flow covered nearby roads and a newly built visitor center, and destroyed the popular local black sand beach. Nevertheless, if you can calm your apprehensions (locals don't seem worried and think New York City is more dangerous), come witness the tremendous power of the earth's miraculous birth process. Walk through extinct lava tubes, drive around the volcano's steaming crater, or, if you are lucky and time it right, survey unforgettable views of flowing red hot lava.

At various times over the past 100 years and in varying intensities, Kilauea has displayed its awesome force in a passionate fury that gurgles up from the earth in rivers and fountains of

2,000-degree molten lava. The thick red fingers move across the land through an array of lava tubes, then spill into the sea in hissing explosions that turn the liquid fire into black powder and rock.

Hotel/Bed and Breakfast Kissing

CARSON'S VOLCANO COTTAGE, Volcano   ●◀
505 Sixth Street
(808) 967-7683
Inexpensive to Moderate

Call for directions.

Surprisingly, you're never without romantic overnight options in Volcano. Carson's Volcano Cottage is one: secluded cabins sheltered in the midst of a lush and overgrown tropical forest. The newly renovated suites are almost too rustic and confining, but still have intriguing detailing: attractive linens, Oriental decor, stained glass windows, and unique art. Some of the cabins even have tiny but private kitchens. All of the rooms include continental breakfast and use of the large, private outdoor Jacuzzi tub.

CHALET KILAUEA, Volcano   ●●◀
Wright Road and Laukapu Road
(808) 967-7786, (800) 937-7786
Inexpensive to Moderate

Call for directions.

Volcano is simply one surprise after another. You'd never expect to find such varied and charming accommodations in this otherwise tiny and drab town. Chalet Kilauea is one of Volcano's hidden treasures: an eclectic two-story rambling cottage, a connecting tree house, and an isolated cabin, all ensconced in the woods. Don't let the main house's slightly shabby exterior and grounds lead you astray; the Oriental decor inside is graciously inviting. Although the three bedrooms share an oddly shaped rustic downstairs bath, the plush detailing of each room (choose from Oriental, African, and European themes) makes them soothing retreats for volcano-weary couples. The adjacent two-level tree-house suite is less ornate, but does provide a private bath (down a flight of outdoor stairs). When the customary late-afternoon fog rolls in, relish complimentary high tea in the common room followed by a dip in the outdoor hot tub.

Walk deeper into the hapu'u forest and you'll discover Chalet Kilauea's most enticing (and most expensive) option: a self-contained, petite cedar cabin with a sunken tub and surrounding windows, rustic yet tasteful decor, and loft bedroom with views of the surrounding woodland. Use of the Jacuzzi and high tea at the nearby main house are included in the price, but even if they weren't this secluded retreat would be worth every penny.

◆ **Romantic Note:** Ask about Chalet Kilauea's three other, less pricey, vacation homes. Again, prices include high tea and use of the Jacuzzi at the main house.

KILAUEA LODGE, Volcano
Volcano Road
(808) 885-4550
Inexpensive to Moderate

Heading north on Highway 11, turn left on Haunani Road and then right onto Volcano Road. The lodge is on the left.

With easily the best restaurant (reviewed elsewhere in this section) in Volcano, Kilauea Lodge offers a full country breakfast that has enticed many to stay at the lodge simply for the food. (Once you've had dinner here, you'll want to book a reservation too.) Fortunately, recent renovations have been made to the lodge itself, bringing the accommodations almost up to par with the outstanding cuisine.

This simple country inn has 12 guest rooms in three adjoining buildings, but we recommend the newer suites in the recently constructed cottage called Hale Aloha. We especially liked the deluxe upstairs honeymoon suite featuring a cathedral ceiling, open beams, king-size bed, fireplace, stained glass window, and private bath. The accommodations in the two original buildings are less fresh and inviting, although they offer genuine country ambience. Fortunately, all of the rooms have central heat, a must for Volcano in the winter.

LOKAHI LODGE BED AND BREAKFAST, Volcano ❖❖
Kalanikoa Road
(808) 885-4550
Inexpensive

Call for directions.

The price is right (we haven't found cheaper) at this country home nestled in the woods, and the welcoming charm of the innkeepers and their lively pets (two dogs and a cat) assures you of a pleasant stay. Although it's nothing fancy, you can experience quiet country living for an extremely agreeable price. The standard-size guest rooms, set off a wraparound lanai, feature private entrances and private baths. All are nicely decorated with colorful country fabrics and down comforters. Complimentary chocolates are left at the bedside for your sweet tooth, and electric heaters are provided (a necessity in the winter). A rather skimpy continental breakfast is served buffet-style in the cozy common room. Still, the home-baked breads are *really* marvelous.

MOUNTAIN HOUSE   ❖❖❖
AND HYDRANGEA COTTAGE, Volcano
(808) 885-4550
Inexpensive to Expensive

Call for address and directions.

Informed romantics know just where to go for real romance in Volcano: among the ohia trees, hapu'u ferns, orchids, magnolias, and hydrangeas of the Mountain House. Nestled in a mountain forest, the once-private estate and an adjacent cottage have been lovingly converted into an elegant bed and breakfast providing guests with sumptuous surroundings and utter seclusion.

Depending on your means, the Hydrangea Cottage can be the better choice of the two. For a phenomenally low price, you get an entire luxury cottage with views of the surrounding woods all to yourselves. The spacious living room has plush modern furnishings, a large kitchen stocked with breakfast foods, extensive windows that allow an infusion of natural light, a wood-burning fireplace, and a VCR (upon request). The bedroom and private bath are equally special. It's hard to believe they don't charge more, but we won't tell them if you won't.

Even more intriguing is the Mountain House, which served as the original home for the owners. Unfortunately, because of their policy, they only rent the house to two couples at a time. You do have the option of paying for the entire house yourselves, but this is *outrageously* expensive, considering the prices of other places in Volcano. You might just want to split the cost and bring along another couple; there's ample room for four. Of interest is the extravagant gourmet kitchen, so large it almost resembles a restaurant. Cook to your heart's content and enjoy the complimentary breakfast already provided for you.

The home's interior is sumptuous and great for lounging, highlighted by koa wood and views of the beautiful surrounding woodland and gardens. The two bedrooms have lovely color schemes and linens, plus private baths, and are situated at opposite ends of the house to ensure privacy. If your budget allows, an evening at the Mountain House might tempt you into staying a day or two longer in Volcano.

Restaurant Kissing

KILAUEA LODGE RESTAURANT, Volcano
Volcano Road
(808) 967-7366
Moderate

Call for directions

People come to Volcano to see the works of Pele the Hawaiian fire goddess, but that doesn't mean they lose their appetites. To tourists' dismay, there are relatively few dining options in Volcano. In fact, the Kilauea Lodge is considered by most not only to be the best, but the *only* dining option here. Despite its lack of competition, the restaurant maintains its reputation by consistently preparing excellent dishes with European and Hawaiian flair.

Cozy up in the provincial dining room next to the Fireplace of Friendship, which hails Kilauea Lodge's past as a YMCA camp with a collection of artifacts from children's groups around the world. Hardwood floors, koa wood tables, fresh flowers, and artistic renditions of Pele's fiery temper enhance your dining enjoyment. Sample fresh local fish or nightly specials such as rack of lamb with apple-papaya-mint sauce. The delightful aromas and flavors are sure to take your mind off the brooding volcano, at least for the moment.

◆ **Romantic Warning:** Avoid the **VOLCANO HOUSE,** located in Hawaii Volcanos National Park, at all costs. Although it is the only other dining option in Volcano, its grim and greasy atmosphere spoils any romantic possibilities.

Outdoor Kissing

HAWAII VOLCANOES NATIONAL PARK,
Volcano

(808) 967-7311
Entrance fee $5 per car.

Heading north on Highway 11, follow the signs to Volcano and then to the park's entrance.

If capricious Kilauea is in a mood to erupt, don't hesitate to witness it for yourself. Without question it is a once-in-a-lifetime event. Unlike any other natural wonder, a volcano moves the soul in a way that is hard to describe.

There are two ways to experience this phenomenon. One is to hike down to the ocean over a well-marked lava field at night to see fountains of molten earth shoot up from the earth (warm clothes, water, snacks, and flashlights are essential). For the less hardy, or those with a more liberal expense account, a helicopter tour is a must. Several flight services will take you aloft to survey the devastation from above it all. (**VOLCANO HELI-TOURS** is one option, (808) 967-7578, about $125 per person.) The pools of bubbling, fiery lava moving through collapsed caverns and open fissures are literally astounding. Sit tight and clasp hands; you're going on the ride of your lives.

> *"Lord! I wonder what fool it was*
> *that first invented kissing."*
>
> Jonathan Swift

Lanai

> *"Her lips on his could tell him better than all her stumbling words."*
> Margaret Mitchell

LANAI

Most of the 7 million visitors who come to Hawaii each year never visit the island of Lanai, and that is one of its most alluring features. A tiny island 18 miles long and 13 miles wide, just 7 miles west of Maui, with a resident population of only 2,400, it has all the tantalizing details of paradise you may be looking for, especially solitude and conspicuous tranquillity. Completing this last frontier are accessible but hard-to-reach sandy beaches where you and your loved one will be the only strollers for miles around, meandering trails to hike, gentle island people who love their land and offer aloha spirit to visitors, truly remote resort hotels with all the sumptuous, accommodating services you would expect from the most elegant of destinations, and no tourist attractions. I'll repeat that because I know it's hard to believe—no tourist attractions. Romance is the very soul of this location.

You won't find the lush vegetation of the other islands here, but every other facet of a blissful tropical paradise awaits. Pine-covered highlands, rocky cliffs, rolling red clay hillsides dabbed with green, and pineapple fields healing from years of operation cover Lanai's arid interior, where little surface water exists to create the lavish rain forests of the other islands. Only one road leads from the boat landing up to Lanai City, 2,000 feet above sea level. This same road meanders around a short distance and splits into two branches that take you to roads accessible by four-wheel-drive vehicles only. Car rentals are expensive ($100 a day), but worth it for a long day's exploration.

Lanai has a fascinating recent history. In the 1920s, 98 percent of the island was purchased by Jim Dole, who developed and planted the illustrious pineapple crop canned by his plantation. For years virtually all of Lanai's usable land was covered in culti-vated fields. Eventually, U.S. costs grew too high, and South America became the new center of pineapple production. The last pineapple harvest here was in 1993. Employment prospects in this

innocent corner of the world would have been devastating had the
Dole Food Company (also flirting with financial woes) not built
two of the most charming, exclusive hotel properties in all of
Hawaii. Now tourism is the major industry on tiny Lanai, with
more controlled development coming.

Is paradise lost? It would be hard to imagine. For now, Dole is the
only developer and they are taking it slow. In the meantime, Lanai
awaits in all of its original glory.

◆   **Romantic Note:** All the inter-island airlines offer flights to
and from Lanai every day. There is also daily passenger-only
ferryboat service from Lahaina, Maui, to Hulope Bay, Lanai, via
EXPEDITIONS, (808) 661-3756. If you take the boat over
between December and March, hang on tight and watch for
whales—they often accompany the crossing.

Lanai City

Hotel/Bed and Breakfast Kissing

THE LODGE AT KOELE, Lanai City
(800) 321-4666, (808) 565-7300
Expensive to Unbelievably Expensive and Beyond

Call for directions and arrival information.

Unlike any other destination in Hawaii, the architecture and
mood at The Lodge at Koele may make you feel you're in the wrong
state. Unmistakable Pacific Northwest flair marks this lodge standing proudly on top of an idyllic verdant hillside. The building
resembles an incredibly luxurious ski lodge, and a casual alpine
spirit envelopes you as you cross the threshold. Outdoors you'll find
immaculate gardens bordered by evergreen forest, with the endless
Pacific in the distance. Centered in the midst of all this lushness are
a large pool and a hot tub.

Inside, the enormous great hall, with its high-beamed ceilings
and two formidable stone fireplaces, is adorned with plush furnishings and fascinating antiques from all over the world. An opulent

Hawaiian plantation feeling is evident in a series of luxurious sitting rooms where guests can have high tea, watch television, or while away the hours playing billiards or other games. A long hallway leads to an adjacent building where each uniquely decorated room is utterly charming and cozy. Four-poster beds, wicker chairs, pine furnishings, large soaking tubs, and private lanais are all affection-inspiring.

Of particular interest are both the Koele Terrace and formal dining room restaurants where sumptuous meals are served with a mastery almost unparalleled on any of the islands. Every meal seemed more remarkable than the last. The menu offers a creative commingling of Mediterranean and Pacific Rim, and every bite is a memorable experience.

THE MANELE BAY HOTEL, Lanai City
(800) 321-4666, (808) 565-7700
Expensive to Unbelievably Expensive and Beyond

Call for directions and arrival information.

You may not know how to describe paradise, but when you see it, you'll know you're there. At The Manele Bay Hotel, in addition to paradise, you'll encounter luxury, grandeur, and gracious, sincere hospitality. From the moment you arrive, unsurpassed attentive service is evident as you are escorted through the magnificent two-story lobby. Towering etched glass doors open out to the grand pool area; in the distance, a rocky bluff outlines the ocean, nearby beach, and pristine countryside. Add to all this exquisite furnishings, poshly decorated dining rooms, a fire-warmed game room, and a variety of stately terraces.

In the guest rooms, European comfort and refinement culminate in serene relaxation. Each large room features expansive sliding glass doors that open to a private lanai overlooking either a sculpted Japanese garden or the pounding surf. Bright yellow English floral fabrics, plantation-style furnishings, and attractive baths further enhance each interior.

The dining rooms are civilized and the food is surprisingly excellent, which is a relief given that they are pretty much the only game in town besides the two dining rooms at The Lodge at Koele. Shuttles are available between the sister properties and the 18-hole panoramic golf course. For superlative solitude and a pampered interlude together, the Manele is every inch a taste of paradise.

◆   **Romantic Note: HOTEL LANAI,** (800) 321-4666, (Inexpensive to Moderate), is the only other available place to stay on Lanai. In comparison to the Manele and the Koele, this is too disappointing for words, but even on its own it isn't anything to write home about. Built in 1923, it has been modestly refurbished. Rooms are small and spartan, with few windows. Its casual restaurant was too smoke-filled for us to eat in, but it seemed on par with everything else—just OK. The price tag is infinitely lower than the other two properties, but that's where its attraction stops.

Molokai

"I don't know how to kiss, or I would kiss you. Where do the noses go?"

Dudley Nichols

MOLOKAI

Molokai has most recently been dubbed "The Friendly Isle," but the former names of "The Forgotten Isle" and "The Lonely Isle" are sadly more appropriate. Unless you're looking for total isolation, Molokai is hard to recommend as a romantic getaway. While detachment from the "real" world can be relaxing, it felt limiting here and the people were anything but friendly. The residents don't encourage tourism for fear that Molokai will become another Oahu, but this doesn't justify the resentful service and general rudeness we encountered.

We were initially let down by the turbulent (understatement) plane ride to the island that revealed dry, barren landscapes and few accessible beaches. The western side of the island is mostly dry, dusty roads, rolling cattle pastures, and former pineapple fields dotted with leafless gray trees and little else.

After driving through miles of parched and lonesome cattle country, the east end of Molokai is a dream come true. Palm trees, which are nowhere else to be found on this island, hem the magnificent rugged coastline, and the surrounding jungle-like countryside is luxuriously thick and green. Beach area is still limited though because the water comes right up to the land, with very little, if any, sand between the ocean and grassy or rocky shores.

It takes nearly an hour to get here from the west end of Molokai (which is where you're likely to be staying), but the dramatic change of scenery and gorgeous views make every second in the car worthwhile. Take turns driving each way so you can both enjoy the view; the narrow, curving road demands all of the driver's attention.

Some of the most dramatic scenery (and intriguing history) is found on the isolated **MAKANALUA PENINSULA**. From a distance, this lovely green peninsula, set beneath Molokai's majestic seaside cliffs (some of the highest in the world) and surrounded by turbulent ocean surf on the remaining three sides, bears no traces of its tragic past. Closer up, mile after mile of gravestones reveal what the peninsula is better known for: the Kalaupapa leper colony. People suffering from leprosy (properly known as Hansen's disease) were first cruelly exiled here by fearful governments in 1866, in attempts to keep the disease under control. People afflicted with Hansen's disease were essentially left here to die and were not provided with even the most basic necessities. In 1873, Father Damien Joseph de Veuster, a Belgian priest who was deeply concerned about the misery of the people at Kalapaupa, settled his ministry here, and brought hope and healing to this lonely peninsula. Father Damien was the first person to recognize the needs of the people at Kalaupapa and spent the remainder of his life serving this community. Today, many refer to Father Damien as a saint and a martyr; sadly, he contracted Hansen's disease himself and died of the disease in 1889.

Thanks to sulfone drugs developed in the 1940s, Hansen's disease is now curable (and not contagious). Yet many recovered patients have chosen to remain in Kalaupapa; today, fewer than 100 people live in this small community. They encourage visitors to learn more about their private peninsula and its past. Despite its somber history, Kalaupapa is a powerful place to behold and a true testament to the strength of the human spirit.

◆   **Romantic Note:** This peninsula is accessible only by foot (it's a steep and strenuous four-hour round-trip hike) or by plane. You are required to call **DAMIEN MOLOKAI TOURS**, (808) 567-6171, for entrance permission. The tour alone is $25; the tour plus plane fare is $80.

The mule rides down to Kalaupapa used to be very popular, but have been put out of business for insurance reasons. Damien Tours hopes to have these back in service soon.

Hotel/Bed and Breakfast Kissing

Maunaloa

PANIOLO HALE, Maunaloa
Kakaako Road
(808) 552-2731, (800) 367-2984
Moderate to Expensive

From the airport, travel west on Highway 460 and turn right at the
Kaluakoi Resort sign. These condos are several miles down; watch
for signs.

After you've followed a long, winding driveway through desolate scenery, Paniolo Hale's well-tended grounds and spacious
condos are a pleasing sight for sore eyes. Each unit is individually
owned and decorated, but all have one noteworthy feature: large,
fully screened-in porches, perfect for letting the blustery trade
winds refresh the rooms.

Some units are decorated more elaborately than others, so if
you're looking for something extra-special and have flexible travel
dates, describe your taste and the staff will gladly accommodate
you. In fact, they were some of the most helpful and pleasant people
we ran into on Molokai.

◆ **Romantic Warning:** As much as we loved this place, we
must mention the bugs. Their explanation of not using pesticides
on the outside spiders because birds eat them made politically
correct sense, but we didn't like the cockroaches we found inside
our condominium.

◆ **Additional Romantic Warning:** If you can't get reservations at Paniolo Hale, stay on Molokai at your own risk. The
other lodging options are tacky, more bug-ridden, and barely
worth considering.

Restaurant Kissing

Dining options on Molokai are limited and certainly not lip-worthy. However, decent meals are served at **JOJO'S**, the only restaurant in the village of Maunaloa, (808) 552-2803, (Inexpensive), where the barbecued ribs and curry are good; the **KUALAPUU COOKHOUSE**, Farrington Road, Kualapuu, (808) 567-6185, (Inexpensive), where you must try the macadamia nut pie; and **MOLOKAI PIZZA**, Wharf Road, Kaunakakai, (808) 553-3288, (Inexpensive), for average pizza on better-than-average crust.

◆ **Romantic Warning:** Don't be fooled by the prime location of the **OHIA LOUNGE**, which revels in glorious sunsets and looks out over the ocean. It is located in the Kaluakoi Resort, 1131 Kaluakoi Road, (808) 552-2721, and is worth mentioning only because you should avoid it. Our servers nearly threw our meals at us and tiny ants paraded on the table throughout dinner.

Halawa

Outdoor Kissing

MOAULA FALLS FOOTPATH

The entrance to this trail is located at the easternmost end of Highway 450.

The footpath begins at a small tumbledown snack shop, whose friendly owners provide maps and parking for $5. You can probably do the hike without the map and park elsewhere, but rental cars on Molokai are prone to theft and it's nice not to have to worry about your belongings. The two-hour (round-trip) hike takes you into the heart of the lush Halawa Valley. Trail markers are sometimes difficult to find, so take it slow and savor the incredible jungle scenery. You feel as if you are in a movie when you finally emerge from the forest and come to the surging waterfall tumbling into a calm green pool of water surrounded by rocks. Share a kiss under the spray of the falls while celebrating your find and swimming together (watch out—it's cold and can be slimy with algae, depending on the season).

◆ **Romantic Warning:** This path is fairly easy to maneuver when it's dry, but can be quite dangerous after a rainfall, due to slippery mud and hidden roots. You have to cross two rivers, an easy skip and a jump over rocks when the water level is low. Excessive rain can bring the water levels knee-deep or higher, which is intimidating, not to mention dangerous. Mosquitoes seem to like this jungle paradise as much as you will, so don't forget bug repellent.

◆ **Romantic Note:** The long drive and walk to the falls might be too tiring for you to try snorkeling in the same day. If you do have energy or care to snorkel another time, stop at **MILEPOST 20,** where a vast reef is full of fish activity. Unfortunately, seclusion is out—everyone seems to know about this small strip of beach that is right along the main highway.

> *"Kisses are like grains of gold or silver found upon the ground, of no value themselves, but precious as showing that a mine is near."*
>
> George Villiers

PERSONAL DIARY

This is a section just for the two of you, so you can keep your own record of the romantic moments you've shared together. Keeping a record of special times, to read when the moment is right, can be an adoring gift, when another romantic outing is at hand.

"*Kissing power is stronger than will power...*"
                                        Abigail Van Buren

> *"Love at the lips was touch*
> *As sweet as I could bear."*
>
> **Robert Frost**

"There are swords about me
to keep me safe:
They are the kisses of your lips."
Mary Carolyn Davies

"I have found men who didn't know how to kiss. I've always found time to teach them."

Mae West

INDEX